The Critical Idiom
Founder Editor: John D. Jump, 1969–76

39 Farce

In the same series

Farce/*Jessica Milner Davis*

Methuen & Co Ltd

First published 1978
by Methuen & Co Ltd
11 New Fetter Lane, London EC4P 4EE
© 1978 Jessica Milner Davis
Typeset by Inforum Ltd, Portsmouth
Printed in Great Britain by
J.W. Arrowsmith Ltd, Bristol

ISBN 0 416 81540 4 (hardbound)
ISBN 0 416 81590 1 (paperback)

Distributed in the USA by
HARPER & ROW PUBLISHERS INC
BARNES & NOBLE IMPORT DIVISION

Contents

Preface

This volume of the Critical Idiom is an attempt to shed some
light upon the genre of farce and the history and usage of the
term in dramatic criticism. Like other subjects in this series,
farce is not easily defined in a few words. The usual compact
definitions found in glossaries and dictionaries are of little help
in distinguishing the farcical from other comic styles. In keeping with the whole concept of the Critical Idiom series, I have
tried to focus broad discussion around a selection of plays readily acknowledged as examples of the farcical genre, hoping in
this way to provide the most concrete illustrations possible of
what characterizes farce in the theatre. In doing so, I have
sought to group these farces into several general categories, so
that the immense range of formal dramatic structures covered
by the genre can be more easily grasped. These classifications
are largely original and they are not proposed dogmatically,
but rather offered in the hope that they may prove useful aids
to further studies of farce.

In the context of contemporary efforts to bypass the institu-
tional theatre with a return to ritual drama and street-mimes,
the psychological functions of farce and its perennial popularity with mimic acting-troupes are topics of some importance.
Is farce an outlet for a conservative and regimented society taking its 'Roman holiday'? Or is it an indulgence only available to
those who can comfortably look back upon the restrictive
social conventions of yesterday? And why is it that the most significant use made of farcical techniques in the twentieth cen-

tury has so far been in the creation of black humour for the Theatre of the Absurd? These and other questions arise directly out of any attempt to deal seriously with this most *non-serious* of types of comedy. Although I cannot answer them, I believe that the answers lie in closer examination of the relationship between the plays themselves and their audiences. The structural analysis of typical farces presented here is a necessary first step in understanding that relationship.

The inspiration for this study was given me by the General Editor of the Critical Idiom, the late John D. Jump. His death in 1976 deprived the series of its founder and guide, and it is to him that I dedicate this volume. My grateful thanks are due especially to Ian Watt of the English Department at Stanford University, to Ken Dutton of the Department of Modern Languages at the University of Newcastle, Australia, and to my husband, Jeremy Davis, all of whom have generously given me their aid in reading and criticizing the typescript. To Janice Price go my thanks for her professional patience and advice.

Stanford, California   *Jessica Milner Davis*

I

What is farce?

> I have not yet seen any definition of Farce, and dare not
> be the first that ventures to define it. I know not by what
> Fate it happens (in common Notion) to be the most
> contemptible sort of Drama. (Nahum Tate, Preface to *A*
> *Duke and No Duke*, edition of 1693)

When the newly created Poet Laureate Nahum Tate set out to
defend farce in 1693, his literary colleagues were accustomed
to employ the word as a term of contempt. Thomas Rhymer,
for example, savagely damned Shakespeare's *Othello* as 'a
Bloody Farce, without salt or savour'. For many people today
farce is still a pejorative term, implying that something is 'as ridiculous as a theatrical farce; . . . a hollow pretence, a mockery'
(*O.E.D.*, s.v. *Farce*, 2). But in the language of criticism, the
word is now generally used in a more constructive sense to identify a particular form of comedy. This the *O.E.D.* succinctly
defines as 'A dramatic work (usually short) which has for its
sole object to excite laughter' (s.v. *Farce*, 1). It is this genre with
which this study is concerned: broad, physical, visual comedy,
whose effects are pre-eminently theatrical and intended solely
to entertain; comedy which is slapstick, if you like, in a more or
less coherently funny narrative; or, as Eric Bentley puts it 'practical joking turned theatrical' (*The Life of the Drama,* N.Y.,
1964, p. 234).

Farce came late to the canon of dramatic terminology.
Unlike the terms comedy, tragedy and even satire, its usage

was not sanctioned by classical authority. In fact, both the Greek and Roman stages seem to have distinguished between various forms of comedy according to their subject-matter, rather than their appropriate comic styles. Thus, Old Comedy was equated with ridicule of individuals, New Comedy with tales of domestic intrigue and adventure, *comoedia palliata* with Greek stories and characters adapted for the Roman stage, *comoedia togata* indicated native Roman characters, and *fabula (comoedia) atellana* described farces with characters and subjects drawn from the rustic town of Atella. What little is known about the antecedents of classical Greek drama, however, suggests that Athenian dramatists of the fifth century B.C. drew upon an earlier tradition of comic village performances, which were popular among the Dorian Greeks, particularly those in the neigbouring province of Megara. Perhaps these were amateur farcical playlets which provided source-material for the more literary drama in the way in which folk-drama informs the work of dramatists the world over. Certainly, to the Athenians Megaran jokes were somewhat low-class and Aristophanes prides himself in his plays on not using 'laughter stolen from Megara'. This did not prevent him, like many other great dramatists, from doing precisely what he denied. In *Wasps*, Xanthias the slave warns the audience:

Don't expect anything profound,
Or any slapstick *à la Megara*.
And we got no slaves to dish out baskets
Of free nuts — or the old ham scene
Of Heracles cheated of his dinner;
... Our little story
Has meat in it and a meaning not
Too far above your heads, but more
Worth your attention than low comedy.
(*Plays*, vol. 1, trans. P. Dickinson, Oxford, 1970, p. 171)

Like Athenian Old Comedy itself, Dorian farce may well

have had its roots in Dionysian festivities. Quite possibly, the ritual invocation of the wine-god and his spirit of fertility called for burlesque impersonation of gods, heroes and even local characters. The act of mimicry often instinctively takes on a comic shape; perhaps by virtue of its licensed status as play, perhaps in acknowledgement of the gap between playful image and serious reality. Protected by the anonymity of costume and mask, mimicry can readily turn to the impersonation of recognizable individuals. In this case, the laughter becomes corrective — an excoriation of social misfits. Aristotle regarded the custom of lampooning in this way as an evolutionary stage in the development of comedy (*Poetics* V 1449b). Roman society possessed a parallel in the abusive 'Fescennine verses', which were improvised at festivals and weddings. Mediaeval Europe too had its *charivari*, or communal procession which mocked in effigy — and sometimes in person — cuckolds, husbands who were beaten by their wives and similar undesirables.

The dangerous tendency towards personal satire is ever-present in the history of farce. Even where mimicry of that kind takes place as part of a licensed festival — during the Feast of Fools, for example, or Carnival, or Twelfth Night — the possibility of giving offence remains. Lampoons, Fescennine verses and *charivari* alike, all exceeded their licence and were actively suppressed by the societies that produced them.

For the primitive comedian seeking to elaborate a fixed, ritual text, more promising ground is offered by exploitation of the illusory nature of his performance itself. His playful mimicry naturally invites the introduction of associate actors who are more (or less) deceived by his act than is his audience. It is no accident that the traditional characters and subjects of the folk-drama — even where it retains a fixed and ritual pattern — have to do with stealing, deception, trickery, magical transformations and practical jokes of all kinds. The English *Mummers' Play*, or the plots of Punch-and-Judy shows, or the exploits of Till Eulenspiegel recorded in the German Carnival-plays, all illustrate this preoccupation. Out of such performances come buffoons who are skilful enough to be worthy of hire and who, in the right economic climate, will create a band of professional entertainers. Inventing their own jokes and patter, they ring the changes upon stock characters and familiar situations, while absorbing new material from literary and political movements of the time. Whenever innovation becomes too controversial for the economic well-being of the troupe, the traditional material can offer a safety-net for their survival.

Such sub-literary, popular entertainment leaves few traces for the historian or sociologist, but it has surfaced repeatedly through the history of the European theatre. The pattern outlined above can be traced, if dimly, in the evolution of the *commedia dell'arte* in sixteenth-century Italy; in the growth of the first professional companies in Spain; in the history of the Elizabethan stage-jig and the hand-to-mouth existence of actors during the Commonwealth period; in the banding together of Parisian *farceurs* at the turn of the sixteenth century; in the early history of the Viennese *Volkstheater*; in the wanderings of the Russian *cabotins*; in the art of the clowns in pantomime and harlequinade and in the varying fortunes of puppeteers and itinerant actors at fairgrounds and street-corners throughout Europe. For the great Russian director, Vsevolod Meyerhold, mime and farce represented the life-springs of the professional theatre from which, even in modern times, it could seek to regenerate itself:

> The idea of the actor's art, based on a worship of mask, gesture and movement, is indissolubly linked with the idea of the farce. The farce is eternal. If its principles are for a time expelled from the walls of the theatre, we nevertheless know that they are firmly engraved in the lines of the manuscripts left by the theatre's greatest writers.   ('Farce', *Theater in*

the Twentieth Century, ed. R.W. Corrigan, N.Y., 1963, pp.205-6)

Farce has certainly always found a ready home in other dramatic forms, whether in between the acts of the literary drama, or as 'comic relief', or merely as one festive element among others within the scope of an all-embracing comedy. The French scholar, Paul Mazon, pointed out the role of Dorian farce in the comedies of Aristophanes as early as 1904 (in his *Essai sur la Composition des Comédies d'Aristophane*, Paris, 1904). Earlier, another French scholar, Gustave Lanson, published an important essay evaluating the contribution of farce and its acting techniques in the comedies of Molière ('Molière et la Farce', *Révue de Paris*, VIII, May, 1901). He dissented from the traditional view that Molière's achievement is cheapened by the influences he absorbed from both the French and the Italian farce traditions. On the contrary, Lanson argued:

> the true Molière is seen in a picture of the Comédia-Française, where he stands amid other illustrious actors of farce, both Italian and French.... These are his masters, these are his origins. And he is great enough not to blush at them.
>
> He is the best *farceur*, and for this reason he is the best creator of comedy. (Trans. Ruby Cohen, *Tulane Drama Review*, VIII, 1963, p.154)

Similar reappraisals have taken the place of other major comic dramatists, including both Plautus in the classical world and Shakespeare in the Renaissance. Allardyce Nicoll, whose pioneering work, *Masks, Mimes and Miracles* (N.Y., 1963), attempted to trace the sub-literary traditions from the classical world through the Dark Ages into mediaeval Europe, reflects this re-evaluation in his treatment of dramatic theory. In the second of his two theoretical studies, farce is regarded as an essential component of a good comedy. He explains:

> When we say that every comedy should be based upon farce, we mean simply that the rough physical framework

provides an excellent skeleton for comedy's richer qualities and that without this it is in danger of becoming too delicate and too refined for theatre's daily food.   (*The Theatre and Dramatic Theory*, London, 1962, p.88)

This kind of approach is of little use, however, in the attempt to come to grips with farce as a genre. As long as it is viewed as existing in symbiosis with 'richer' forms of comedy, farce can only be characterized by negatives — the more exaggerated characterizations, the cruder coincidences and the grosser pieces of joking belong to the farce, while the more sophisticated elements of plot, character and theme are those of comedy proper. Throughout its history, critics have tended to see farce in this negative light and to dismiss it as a genre with brief descriptions such as Nicoll's 'rough physical framework', or 'gross and improbable characterization', 'horse-play and slap-stick'. For L.J. Potts, farce is 'comedy with the meaning left out; which is as much as to say, with the comedy left out' (*Comedy*, London, 1949, p.37). Many critical works on types of the drama do not even bother to define what is meant by farce; and those that do, rarely do so with objectivity. In 'A Note on Farce' (*Quarterly Journal of Speech*, XLVI, 1960), J.D. Hurrell observes that 'farce, having once been relegated to the lowest level of the series headed by tragedy, has continually been taken for granted as something if not actually beneath criticism, at least beneath the need for critical discussion' (p.426). Examining the entry on farce in the authoritative *Oxford Companion to the Theatre* (ed Phyllis Hartnoll, Oxford, 1951), Eric Bentley concludes that 'the whole article is based on the assumption . . . that farce consists of defects without qualities' ('The Psychology of Farce', *'Let's Get a Divorce!' and Other Plays*, p.viii).

When farce is examined for its own sake in the context of plays which make no claim to be anything *other* than farce, its formal parameters can more easily be grasped. In France during the late Middle Ages, farce actually achieved this structural independence and was both named and recognized as a distinct dramatic type. In the ensuing centuries, however, farce has so often played an adjunct role in the theatrical bill that confusion over its characteristics has continued to reign.

Being short and often episodic in structure, farce is by nature suited to this role of 'filling'. Indeed, its name is actually derived from the Latin *farcire*, 'to stuff', and the word 'farce' remains in both French and English a rather old-fashioned name for a stuffing for meat and other foods. Its first connection with the drama seems to have come by absorption of the verb-form into ecclesiastical usage. In the period between the ninth and twelfth centuries, the Latin liturgy of the Church underwent a process of musical and verbal enrichment by the addition of tropes, or embellishing phrases. Those phrases and their musical accompaniment which were inserted into parts of the Mass, such as the Kyrie and the Sanctus, were often called *farsae* or *farsurae*. The term was also used for the reading of Lessons and Epistles which had been 'farced' in this way. In French and Italian cathedrals by the beginning of the twelfth century these *farsurae* were often composed in the vernacular, as a gloss on the meaning of the Latin passages being chanted to the congregation from the scriptures set for a particular day. *Épitres farcies* ('farced epistles') were used, for example, on the Feast of St Stephen and on Christmas Day, presumably with the aim of helping the people to understand the events lying behind the story of the first Christian martyr and the birth of the Saviour.

This 'farced' material was not, of course, farcical. But, interestingly, at this same period, the process of 'troping' was also taking on dramatic form. Tropes representing the visit of the shepherds and the Magi to the Christmas crib and that of the Marys to the empty tomb at Easter were enacted as a regular part of the liturgy for the appropriate feasts as early as the tenth century in monasteries such as Winchester, Fleury, St

Gall, Benediktbeuern and Limoges. By the twelfth century, these liturgical dramas were also making use of the vernacular, as well as Latin, for their chanted dialogue and some plays had either outgrown their place in the liturgy or were composed specially for performance in their own right.

There is no evidence that the term *farsa* was used in reference to these plays. The usual term for those which remained part of the liturgy was *Ordo* (service), or *Officium* (office). Where a play had independent status, it might be called *ludus* (play), or *spiel, jeu* or *auto*, for those in German, French or Spanish vernacular languages. Some critics have thought that 'farcing' may have related to the introduction of comic business in the form of vernacular dialogue interpolated into the sober, Latin plays. This theory is not borne out by the historical development of the plays, however. The earliest passages in the vernacular are by no means characteristically comic. They serve rather to introduce 'human interest' in the central story — Mary's lament at the foot of the cross, for example, or Mary Magdalene's dancing-song as she attracts the attention of her admirers, or the chant of the soldiers on watch outside the Tomb. Dramas composed entirely in the vernacular are contemporaneous with Latin dramas, moreover, and comic scenes such as the raging of Herod, or the exploits of devils garnering the damned souls for Hell, were not necessarily marked by use of the vernacular.

It seems likely, nevertheless, that the process of 'farcing' acquired some connection with entertainment. Among other feasts at which *épitres farcies* ('farced epistles') were prescribed was the 'Feast of Fools' (also known as the 'Feast of the Ass'). In France, this developed into a riotous celebration which required reform by the end of the twelfth century. Records from the cathedral-schools of Beauvais and Sens give some idea of the extraordinary nature of this Saturnalian feast, which took place as the culmination of Christmas revels on the Feast of the Circumcision (1 January). From the Feast of St

Stephen (26 December) onwards, in ecclesiastical communities, various ranks of the clergy were permitted their special day of indulgence; on the Feast of the Holy Innocents (28 December) for example, a Boy Bishop from the choristers might be elected to rule over the festivities. The Feast of the Circumcision was the day of the despised sub-deacons, who contributed the greatest disruption to the established order. At Beauvais, an ass was escorted in procession up the nave of the cathedral by canons bearing wine while the burlesque 'Prose of the Ass' was sung; the censing at Mass was done with black puddings and sausages; the celebrant was instructed to bray three times to conclude the service, while the congregation responded similarly. Sir E. K. Chambers described the ruling idea of the Feast as 'the inversion of status, and the performance, inevitably burlesque, by the inferior clergy of functions properly belonging to their betters'(*The Mediaeval Stage*, vol. I, Oxford, 1903, p.325). More widely, it was an opportunity to celebrate freedom from normal discipline and to mock those sober souls who resisted this topsy-turvy reign by the 'fools', or devotees of the ass. And it undoubtedly involved masking and mimicry.

The whole Christmas period, covering the winter solstice and corresponding roughly with the Roman *Saturnalia* (which in pagan times had been celebrated on 17 December) and the Kalends (1-3 January), was of course one of merrymaking and misrule. Both the institution of the *Rex Saturnalis* and the temporary exchanges of roles between master and man, which characterized the Kalends, can clearly be traced in Christmas festivities, even today (see Donaldson, *The World Upside-Down*, pp.15-16). In mediaeval England, the milder indulgences of the Feast of the Boy Bishop were more common, although the Feast of Fools was not unknown. But in France, the activities of the licensed fools, or *sots*, were so popular with the laity as well as with the junior clergy, that, when the religious feast was forbidden in 1438, the townsfolk took it over and formed their own secular societies of *sots* to perpetuate the reign of folly. The professional guild of law-clerks known as the 'Basoche' was instrumental in forming these *compagnies joyeuses* ('merry companies'), or *sociétés des fous* ('societies of fools'), as they were called. In the hand of these educated young men, the mimicry and satirical play-making associated with the Feast expanded greatly.

By the end of the fourteenth century, the organization and acting of religious drama was largely in the hands of lay societies. In England, these were the trade-guilds who presented plays over several days at the Feast of Corpus Christi. In Italy and Spain, they were the charitable associations known as *compagnie* and *cofradiás* respectively. In France, however, specialized *confrèries* ('fraternities') were formed, some to honour particular saints by dramatizing their lives and miracles. In 1402, the *Confrèrie de la Passion* in Paris ('Brotherhood of the Passion') was granted monopoly within the city to perform religious drama. Although the evidence is sketchy, it seems that the members of religious *confrèries* and the *sots* (or *fous*) or of *societes joyeuses* might agree to combine their talents in staging religious plays. There was certainly an understanding of this kind between the *Confrèrie de la Passion* and the *sots* of the powerful Parisian branch of the Basoche, who called themselves *Les Enfants sans souci* ('The Carefree Children').

The division of acting skills which was recognized by such agreements in France accompanied a differentiation in dramatic structure which is unparalleled elsewhere in Europe. Texts from the early fifteenth century show that a typical French religious play — a *mystère* (mystery) or a *vie de saint* (saint's life) — might very well include a comic episode which was explicitly intended as comic relief. A manuscript dated c. 1420, for example, which quite possibly formed part of the repertoire of the *Confrèrie de la Passion*, contains a series of plays about the miracles performed by Saint Geneviève. At the head of one *Miracle* a forthright textual direction reads:

Miracles de plusiers malades
En farses pour etre mains fades.
(*Mystères Inédits du 15e Siècle*, ed. A. Jubinal, Paris, 1837,
p.281)

(More miracles of [healing] the sick
Done with farces to be less dull.)

Among the monologue complaints of various victims who present themselves to be healed by the saint is a short scene between a blind man and his guide — a scabrous and deceitful boy named Hannequin. After some cruel leg-pulling, the pair also join the queue waiting for the saint and are duly healed in mind and body when she passes by.

A much earlier manuscript (dating from 1266) contains a similar scene of crude farce known as *Le Garçon et l'Aveugle (The Boy and the Blind Man)* and set in the Tournai region of France. Its existence suggests that this playlet was traditionally popular and may well have been performed by wandering professional mimes. The inclusion of the traditional characters in this *Miracle* must certainly have demanded skilled comic acting, if its aim of attracting the audience's flagging attention was to be fulfilled.

In other religious plays, similar kinds of comic episode are also referred to as 'farsses' or 'farces'. In the case of a *Mystère de St Eloi (Mystery of Saint Eloi)* played at Dijon in 1447, which was the subject of a law suit, the court records affirm that 'pardedans ledit mystère y avoit certaine farce meslée par manière de faire reveiller au rire les gens' ('in the middle of the said mystery there was a certain farce, put in so that it would excite the people to laughter', Petit de Julleville, *Répertoire du Théâtre Comique en France au Moyen-âge*, Paris, 1886, p.330). The complaint brought before the court was that the audience had been excited to laughter against the King and the Dauphin by political references in this *farce*.

Perhaps it was problems of this kind which brought about

the generic distinction between the *farce* and the *sottie* as the two kinds of comic performance given by the *compagnies des fous*. The *sottie* was an allegorical satire, in which the actors, dressed as *sots* in their parti-coloured costumes with cap and bells, set out to demonstrate the truth of the motto, 'stultorum numerus est infinitus' ('the number of fools is infinite'). The biting political satire of unmasking the *sot* behind every public and private figure provided the dramatic climax for the *sottie*; but inevitably, such satire constantly provoked official reaction, the imprisonment and punishment of actors and finally, in the mid-sixteenth century, the suppression of all fool societies. The *farce*, on the other hand, embodied a more tolerant attitude towards man's stupidity. Restricting itself to a more generalized kind of comic mimicry, it proved a more long-lasting vehicle for lively fun. The masterpieces of this genre, such as the *Farce du Cuvier (Farce of the Washtub*, c. 1500; see Chapter 3) and the famous *Farce du Maître Pierre Pathelin* (c. 1480; almost certainly a Basoche-farce) have made the type familiar. A short, uproarious plot presents a comically balanced struggle for power between two opposing forces — husband and wife, parent and child, master and thief — whose characterization is convincingly realistic and down-to-earth.

The nature of this kind of comedy was recognizably farcical in the modern sense to the French critic Thomas Sebillet when he described it in 1545. For him, it corresponded to the Latin mimes in its licence and laughter and lack of formal structure. Its true subject-matter was 'badineries, nigauderies et toutes sotties esmouvantes à ris et plaisir' ('bantering, tomfoolery and every kind of idiocy that can give rise to laughter and amusement', *Art Poétique François*, ed. F. Gaiffe, Paris, 1910, p.165). Fifty years later, a French manual on literary practice gave advice that still rings true in the twentieth century:

Le suject [de la farce] doit estre gay et de risée; il n'y a ny scenes ni pauses. Il faut noter qu'il n'y a pas moins de science

à scavoir bien faire une farce qu'une eglogue ou
moralité. (P. Delaudun d'Aigaliers, *L'Art Poétique François*. Paris, 1598, s.v. *Farce*)
(The subject [of farce] must be merry and laughable; there
are neither scene divisions nor pauses. It should be noted
that there is no less science in knowing how to make a good
farce than an eclogue or a morality play.)

That these *farces* remained popular after the demise of the
sociétés joyeuses is shown by the large number of them which
passed into print during the sixteenth century. They became a
drawcard for the elaborate communal productions of religious
drama — at Seurre, for example, in 1496, when it rained, the
audience gathered for the show was persuaded to stay and wait
for fine weather by being offered a *farce*. Increasingly, the
farces and the roles for the *fou* (or madman) which were
inserted into the religious drama seem to have attracted (or
required) the talents of professional actors, as well as those of
the expert, semi-professional *sots*. In 1545, a legal contract of
agreement was signed by members forming a travelling troupe
to play 'moralites, farces et autres jeux roumains et françois'
('moralities, farces and other Latin and French plays') (G.
Cohen, *Histoire de la mise en scène dans le théâtre religieux
français*, 2nd edn, Paris, 1926, p.204). For the earliest acting-
troupes in France farce thus formed a livelihood, and it was in
this school that Molière and his colleagues were trained.

In both France and Italy, patrons at court demanded for
their entertainment a refined, literary comedy which would
observe the neo-classical rules of structure and decorum. In
Italy, where this kind of comedy was called the *commedia eru-
dita* ('learned comedy'), *farsa* was the recognized term for a
loose genre, neither tragedy nor comedy nor pastoral, which
could be easy-going precisely because it lacked classical antecedents. Using the conventional image of his work as his mistress, the dramatist Giovan-Maria Cecchi praised the 'new'

genre in an enthusiastic prologue to his play, *La Romanesca (The Roman Girl,* 1585):

> The *Farsa* is a new third species between tragedy and comedy. It enjoys the liberties of both, and shuns their limitations . . . . It is not restricted to certain motives; for it accepts all subjects — grave and gay, profane and sacred, urbane and rude, sad and pleasant. It does not care for time or place . . . . In a word, this modern mistress of the stage is the most amusing, the most convenient, the sweetest, prettiest, country-lass that can be found upon our earth. (Trans. J.S. Kennard, *The Italian Theatre*, vol. I, N.Y., 1932, p.179.)

A very similar understanding of the term was current at this time in Spain, where, before the establishment of the term *comedia* (meaning a play) in the seventeenth century, *farsa* was simply one of several words for a dramatic performance. *Auto sacramentale* ('sacred play') and *farsa sacramentale* were interchangeable.

Such a free-and-easy genre exactly suited the professional acrobats and buffoons who offered themselves for hire by city authorities, academies and noble households in Italian city-states in the early sixteenth century. Unlike the members of literary academies, amateur playwrights and actors who composed and performed *commedie erudite*, the skill of the professional *comici* ('comedians') lay in improvization. As the fame of their acting grew, their style of comedy became known throughout Europe as the *commedia dell'arte* ('the comedy of the skill, or the art'; hence, 'the professional comedy'). For their plots, the *comici* drew indiscriminately from literary and classical comedy, from *novelle* and romances, from traditional village pastimes and their own skills in acrobatics and mimicry.

Performances of the *commedia dell'arte* depended upon each actor memorizing an outline, or *scenario*, and developing his improvizations within its scope and in co-ordination with his colleagues. The actor was also governed by his role, which did not change from play to play, since the characters of the *commedia* were fixed, although their social role might vary. An actor chose his traditional character, or 'mask', and developed it to suit his personality. Each had its own repertoire to be memorized: dialogues, typical behaviour, pieces of business, or 'lazzi', standard jokes, or 'burle', set speeches, orations and acrobatic turns. According to his talents, the individual actor added his own inventions. The characters of the *commedia* were partly archetypal, partly original and fantastic creations. There were the impotent old fathers, such as Pantalone the miser, or the learned il Signor Dottore; the languishing ladies, wives or daughters; the buxom servant girls; the smooth and potent lovers; the braggart captains; and the pairs of clownish servants, who, between them, would provide enough wits to concoct a plot and enough stupidity to confuse it. Most of these roles were played using individualized masks or half-masks so that the acting was necessarily highly stylized.

Given type-characterization and mimic acting, the plots of the *commedia dell'arte* tended naturally to broad comedy, rather than to complex psychological drama. Intrigue and buffoonery demand detached laughter or distant and magical romance, rather than empathy and human insight. The skill of the actors lay in presenting the audience with a visual mixture of mental rigidity and acrobatic elasticity which has never since been paralleled. In this sense, the *commedia dell'arte* was an elaborate dramatization of the most fundamental of all practical jokes: the joke that man's spirit is trapped within and must express itself through man's body. Perhaps because of this, the name of the *commedia* is sometimes regarded as synonymous with farce. Its plots, however, like those of the early *farsa*, were not restricted to farce and in later periods particularly, romance, scenic spectacle and topical satire were an important part of the *commedia dell'arte's* phenomenal popularity. From the end of the sixteenth century onwards, troupes of *comici* paid regular visits to Spain, Vienna, Paris and London. In 1680, a permanent company was established by royal decree at the Hotel de Bourgogne in Paris — the Comédie Italienne. Italian actors were still performing at the Opéra Comique in the late eighteenth century. The impact of the *commedia dell'arte*, both in acting style and in traditional masks and themes, made itself felt throughout Europe.

Although farce was not known by that name in sixteenth-century England, it was thoroughly familiar in practice to audiences and actors alike. Broad comedy and clowning had formed an integral part of mediaeval and Tudor drama and comedians such as Richard Tarleton and Will Kempe, who composed and performed their own jests and farces, were leading members of the first adult acting companies. The Elizabethan stage developed, in fact, its own form of 'comic stuffing' — the stage-jig, a mimed dance with dialogue which was sung to popular tunes. The jig took audiences by storm, both in England and in Germany and Scandinavia, where visiting English companies toured with great success at the turn of the century. When Randle Cotgrave compiled and printed an English/ French dictionary in 1611, he well understood the similarity of function between French *farce* and the contemporary jig. With a nod to Puritan opinion, he described a *farce* as 'a (fond [i.e. foolish] and dissolute) Play, Comedie, or Enterlude; also, the Iyg at the end of the Enterlude, wherein some pretie knauerie is enacted' (*A Dictionary of the French and English Tongues*, s.v. *Farce*).

In the face of Cromwell's efforts to destroy the theatre as an institution, the strength and popularity of this comic tradition helped to sustain its actors. Such illegal performances as could take place during the Commonwealth period were chiefly of brief farces or 'drolls', as they were called. They were played in secrecy and haste at fairgrounds and in theatres which were supposed to be closed. Texts of jigs and abbreviated comic scenes drawn from Elizabethan and Jacobean plays illustrate the repertoire of this period from 1642 to the Restoration of the Crown in 1660.

After the Restoration, many French influences were brought to bear upon the fashionable world of the newly opened theatres. Among them was the use of the word 'farce'. Both the term itself and the kind of comedy it denoted were regarded as characteristically foreign — part French, part Italian, under the impact of the *commedia dell'arte*. Like other foreign commodities, farce was novel, chic, amusing, probably decadent and certainly daring. Some dramatists, like Nahum Tate, never quite part of the literary establishment despite his later appointment as Poet Laureate, welcomed the new genre for its flexibility and popular appeal. But to the conservative arbiters of taste, who regarded popular applause as fickle and debased, farce was to be condemned. John Dryden must have spoken for many aspiring literary dramatists when, in the Preface to his play *An Evening's Love* (1671), he deplored the fact that 'as the Artist is often unsuccessful, while the Mountebank succeeds; so Farces more commonly take the people than comedies' (London, 1671, A4ᵛ).

Although the discipline of farce is certainly extra-literary, its requirements are strict. Paradoxically, the crudest of all comic forms is a demanding, even a challenging style for dramatist and actor alike. From the correct reception of custard pies to the precise machinery of a complex display of fireworks by Georges Feydeau, the masterly French *farceur* of the last century, it is the physical skills of the actor, and the corresponding visual imagination of the dramatist, which are at a premium. Verbal and literary artifice is simply overwhelmed by physical action in farce. Dryden's elitist spirit was bound to disapprove of the genre; and perhaps the theatrical technique of his comedies suffered accordingly.

Another complaint voiced by Dryden and many other dramatists was founded on a kind of chauvinistic pride. They saw the vogue for farce threatening to stifle the originality of English comedy, as a spate of French and Italianate adaptations reached the stage. In the Prologue to *The Conquest of Granada* (1670), Dryden attempted to sway opinion to his side by rousing national pride:

> May those drudges of the Stage, whose fate
> Is damn'd dull Farce more dully to translate,
> Fall under that excise the State thinks fit
> To set on all French wares, whose worst, is wit.
> French farce worn out at home, is sent abroad;
> And patch'd up here is made our English mode.

But whatever the opinions of Dryden and other critics, public taste was not to be denied. Farces, both native and French in inspiration, established themselves in the repertoire. Such was the sucesss of the 'new' genre, that its name became synonymous with pure hilarity. When Dryden himself, in association with the Duke of Newcastle, produced an enormously popular comedy (which is certainly farcical, if not farce), *The Feign'd Innocence, or, Sir Martin Marr-All* (1667), the diarist Pepys described it in the following terms:

> It is the most entire piece of mirth, a complete farce from one end to the other, that certainly ever was writ. I never laughed so in all my life. I laughed till my head [ached] all the evening and night with the laughing; and at very good wit therein, not fooling. The house full.   (*Pepys on the Restoration Stage,* Helen Macfee, Yale U.P., 1916, p.202)

Throughout the history of the theatre, farce has proved itself in this way with its audiences and its perennial appeal has largely ignored critical disdain.

Towards the end of the seventeenth century, under the rule of William and Mary, economic pressures upon the theatre began to make themselves felt in a new way. In 1714, a second London theatre opened — Lincoln's Inn Fields — in competition with Drury Lane and, as a result, the entertainment power of farce acquired a new significance. The farce-afterpiece became a regular part of the theatrical bill. Although many kinds of dramatic novelties were used for the afterpiece — acrobatic and scenic spectacles, comic and pastoral operettas, for example — farce provided the mainstay.

The vogue which developed during the course of the eighteenth century for sentimental comedies and for tragi-comedy merely strengthened the position of farce on the bill as a counter-balance. In his *Dissertation ... on the Provinces of Dramatic Poetry*, Bishop Hurd remarked that farce distinguished itself from other mixed forms of comedy precisely by this robust quality, explaining that its 'sole aim and tendency . . . is to excite laughter' (*Works*, vol. 2, London, 1811, p.30). The afterpiece of this period is typically concerned with a boisterous love intrigue, in which the interest lies more in the tricks and treachery by which the young lovers manage to have their own way, than in any romantic languishings on their part. It was not uncommon, however, for a popular afterpiece to be lengthened into a more sentimental mainpiece; while a five-acter which dragged could be truncated and 'farcicalized' (the comedy broadened and made more visual) to form a suitable afterpiece. The dividing-line between this intrigue-farce and the full-scale comedy of manner is clearly rather fine and reveals a constant tension between sentiment and foolery. In the work of Sheridan and Goldsmith, the comedy of manners achieved a triumphant resolution of these opposing forces, in which a romantic and humane approach to the central figures of the lovers is harmoniously combined with robust clowning.

As the proportion of working and professional people among the audience continued to increase during the nineteenth century, the content of the repertoire gradually reflected this demographic shift. Relevance of subject-matter affected farce as well as serious drama. From the period of the 1840s onwards, farces gradually abandoned aristocratic young lovers and their scheming servants, in favour of the everyday lives of working men and women. Their fun is derived from the way in which the normal train of domestic events is transformed into a whirlwind of confusions and mistaken identities. Despite the stylized slapstick, these pieces, like the famous *Box and Cox* by J.M. Morton (1847) (which is also well known in W.S. Gilbert's version as *Cox and Box*), are thoroughly English in character and setting. They share with earlier farces that blunt, native tradition which had aptly been characterized by Dryden's contemporary, Thomas Shadwell, as a concern with 'the Putting out of candles, kicking down of Tables, falling over Joynt-stools, impossible accidents and unnatural mistakes' (Dedication to his *A True Widow*, 1679).

Towards the end of the nineteenth century, however, the influence of the more sexually sophisticated, contemporary Parisian farce began to make itself felt. The theatre of the Palais Royal in Paris made a name for itself by specializing in farces which dealt quite explicitly with sexual themes. One of its leading dramatists was Eugène Labiche and in 1873 his well-known *Chapeau de Paille d'Italie (The Italian Straw Hat)* was presented in London, adapted by W.S. Gilbert as *The Wedding March*. In 1874, London actor-manager Charles Wyndham offered a rather daring piece by Bronson Howard and Frank Marshall entitled *Brighton*, which featured a hero whose mechanical habit was to make love to every female in sight. In 1877 Wyndham offered the even more racy *Pink Dominos* (an adaptation of *Les Dominos Roses* by A.N. Hennequin and A.L. Delacour). The review by the *Daily Telegraph* contributed notably to the instant success of the new piece. Its notice began:

All who know anything of the Parisian stage are aware of the kind of pieces usually associated with the Palais Royal, and everybody desirous of maintaining the purity of the drama in this country must have regretfully noticed that a theatre in Piccadilly has seemed lately to emulate the distinction acquired by that establishment. (*Daily Telegraph*, 5 April 1877)

A spate of English adaptations and translations of French farce followed, each dealing with the dubious adventures of highly respectable characters who, for the most understandable of reasons, have been tempted to venture beyond their normal haunts and thus to risk their reputations in suspicious circumstances. G.B. Shaw, who despised all farce for its lack of social conscience and for its mechanical laughter, summarized the typical three-act structure of the genre at this time:

> I first learnt the weariness of it from Pink Dominos, although that play had an excellent third act; and I have been wearied in the same way by every new version. For we have had it again and again under various titles. Act 1, John Smith's home; Act II, the rowdy restaurant or casino at which John Smith, in the course of his clandestine spree, meets all the members of his household, including the schoolboy and the parlourmaid; Act III, his house the next morning, with the inevitable aftermath of the complications of the night before: who that has any theatrical experience does not know it all by heart? (*Our Theatre in the Nineties*, vol. II, London, 1932, p.120)

In the hands of Pinero and Wilde the conventional formula nevertheless achieved a brilliance and a polish which have immortalized pieces like *The Magistrate* (1885), *Dandy Dick* (1887) and *The Importance of Being Ernest* (1895).

In a crusading spirit, Shaw set out to convert the techniques of farce to what he considered a valid dramatic purpose. His aim was to 'humanize' the conventionally heartless materials and to lift his audiences above mere thoughtless entertainment. The results, in *You Never Can Tell* (1899) and *Getting Married* (1908), for example, are fascinating but uncertain, with the dramatic action shifting awkwardly from farce to pathos to intellectual discussion and back to farce again. Audiences at the time seem to have found it easier to respond to the powerful and familiar conventions, rather than to the veneer of rationalization; so that, as usual, Shaw found his intentions misunderstood. In his attitude to farce, however, he is not alone. Many literary critics have joined in the complaint that farce lacks either meaning or emotion. Shaw classed 'the laughter produced by conventional farcical comedy as purely galvanic, and the inference drawn by the audience that since they are laughing they must be amused or edified or pleased, as a delusion' (*Our Theatre in the Nineties*, vol. II, pp.119-20). To him, farce was merely a rarefied but not very refined form of malicious pleasure at the sufferings of others. He declared:

> To laugh without sympathy is a ruinous abuse of a noble function; and the degradation of any race may be measured by the degree of their addiction to it. In its subtler forms it is dying very hard: for instance, we find people who would not join in the laughter of a crowd of peasants at the village idiot, or tolerate the public flogging of a criminal, booking seats to shout with laughter at a farcical comedy, which is, at bottom, the same thing — namely, the deliberate indulgence of that horrible, derisive joy in humiliation and suffering which is the beastliest element in human nature.   (*Our Theatre in the Nineties*, vol. II, London, 1932, p.118)

What Shaw's idealistic viewpoint led him to overlook, and what his 'humanized farces' missed time and again, was the essential human predicament embodied in crude farce. Comedy is drawn from the most human of strivings: our continual impulse to rebel against convention and morality and our continued efforts to master our own bodies and our physical environment. Most often, the joke entails the failure of the attempt; but it is a failure which must also touch the audience, since the joke is on us all as members of the human race. And sometimes the joke is an unexpected success, although the success is as much beyond individual control as was the original impulse to rebellion. Farce does not deny that human aspirations exist: it merely regards them as a joke.

It is understandable that critics like Shaw, who make heavy intellectual demands upon the theatre, can only find contempt for the non-serious purposes of farce and its audiences. But there is a paradoxical value in farce's wild rejection of the laws of rationality and seriousness. Farce enshrines the element of unreason, an admittedly important part of human nature. From the Feast of Fools to the Marx Brothers, farce permits an indulgent regression to the joys and terrors of nonsense. With more weight being given to psychological factors, contemporary criticism is now beginning to identify the correct value of farce. A recent book by Morton Gurewitch puts this point of view enthusiastically:

> The victories of farce do not honor the accomplishments of human reason; instead, they register vital revolts against reason's heavily regulative hand — and against all other onerous requirements of civilization.
>
> For those who view comedy chiefly as an adjunct of critical insight or rational progress, farce will doubtless always signify low aspirations. Even defenders of farce are often reluctant to claim that it is an art-form which rightly disrupts civilized dignity, responsibility, and guilt.
>
> (*Comedy: the Irrational Vision*, Cornell U.P., 1975, p.234)

There is, nevertheless, some danger in a hasty celebration of farce's unreason: that of overlooking the structure by which the release from rationality is achieved. A farce is no mere medley of inane japes and bacchanalian hoots. Its illogicality is most logical. Dryden and Shaw correctly perceived the repetitive and mechanical nature of farce-plots, although they may have ignored the possibilities for powerful comic effect inherent in such material. Farce is indeed mechanical and its mechanical manipulations of plot and character distinguish it clearly from other, more flexible comic forms. Like all comedy, farce is both aggressive and festive. At its heart is the eternal comic conflict between the forces of conventional authority and the forces of rebellion. But since farce, more than other comic forms, depends upon the direct, dramatic enactment of its jokes and humiliations, it is in more danger of becoming merely and violently aggressive. The strictness of its rules is necessary to prevent farce from over-balancing into an outright attack upon social conventions of its time. If the farcical conflict is released from its traditional patterns of balance, farce becomes dangerous and liable to provoke the response of censorship. If the conflict is allowed to escape its stylized and care-free 'play-frame', farce becomes cynical, a piece of black, absurdist comedy. If it is provided with characters who are self-conscious about the wrongs they inflict and suffer, farce becomes pathetic, a tragical romance, which can only be recalled to comedy by an unlooked-for happy ending.

The simplest of farcical structures display clear signs of this attention to balance and patterning, to the stylization of acting and to the depersonalization of character. In the following chapters, I shall discuss several different levels of complexity in conventional farce-structures. The concluding chapter will examine what happens when those conventions are broken and farcical structures become the media for dramatic messages other than farce. The wide range from which examples are drawn is an attempt to illustrate the ancient lineage of farce as a genre; but the reader should be warned that the order in which plays are discussed bears little relation to their chronology.

2

The world of rebellion

> See how this man disturbs the whole order of society to
> further his joking; how scandalously he inverts the most
> sacred relationships upon which society is founded; how
> he turns to mockery the revered rights of fathers over
> their children, of husbands over their wives, of masters
> over their servants! He creates laughter, it is true, and
> only makes himself the more culpable for doing so.
> (J-J. Rousseau on Moliere, *Lettre à M. D'Alembert sur
> les Spectacles*, in OEuvres, vol. II, p.44, my translation)

The simplest kind of farce requires little more than a suitable
victim, a practical joker and a good idea for a prank. Given
these, the joke, or 'burla' as the artists of the *commedia dell'
arte* called it, needs no further excuse for existence. As K.M.
Lea observes in her study, *Italian Popular Comedy*, one clown
merely says to the other, 'Let's do the old man' or, 'Let's do him
again' and the farce moves forward. At this level, farce is very
little removed from ordinary circus clowning, in which uncon-
nected episodes are motivated solely by the availability of a
defenceless or gullible victim, without any particular purpose
being served by his humiliation.

Psychologists would term this 'hostile' or 'aggressive' joking.
It constitutes exactly that aspect of farce which repulsed Shaw
as being 'uncivilized and primitive', a childish delight in the
bad luck of others less powerful, or less lucky, than oneself.
Farce is unquestionably hostile and its joking goes far beyond
the malicious innuendo and derogation found in such 'hostile'
verbal jokes, as for example, '"What would happen if the Krem-

lin took over the Sahara Desert?" Answer: "In a year there would be a shortage of sand".' In a farce, the victim is shown both inviting and suffering ridicule, and the insult is delivered directly and physically to the person of the victim. The message of hostility between two individuals is fully acted out.

The psychological satisfactions and perhaps the benefits of farce lie chiefly in the deliberate offence it gives to social norms. Where victims 'ask for' punishment by their stupidity, they are tortured shamelessly; where they provoke retaliation by their role as 'kill-joys', they are often people whose humiliation would outrage social conventions — representatives of authority and propriety. Yet, as Shaw complains, normally decent people see nothing wrong in enjoying a farce of this kind: comic mayhem is what they expect when they go to see a farce.

In his study of *Jokes and their Relationship to the Unconscious* (originally published in 1904) Freud pointed out that the fantasies of humour, like those of dreams, bypass taboos established by our innate 'cultural censor'. The fantasies permit more primitive, underlying impulses to express themselves in ways which both our conscious and our unconscious minds would habitually forbid. We regress to forms of pleasure which are normally inhibited and rejected as childish, as uncivilized or possibly even as 'sinful'. Jokes permit the delights of nonsense-talk, of what Freud calls 'smut', or free reference to sexual and anal functions, a vicarious indulgence of the body and all its senses; and give free rein to hostility against the curbs demanded by proper social behaviour.

Two complementary elements are at work in this process, the impulse to pleasure and self-indulgence and the impulse to aggression and hostility. Perhaps at bottom these two elements are one. Some psychologists would argue that man is endowed with an independent instinct for aggression which it is pleasing to satisfy in one way or another. Others, more sanguine, believe that man is not aggressive until frustrated when he desires to retaliate against those responsible for the frustration. Whichever view of human nature is taken, the pleasure of joking is clearly partly festive and indulgent, partly aggressive and hostile.

Interestingly enough, such a combination of elements, festive and aggressive, has been shown to characterize the fertility rituals which lie at the root of dramatic comedy. Early studies by Francis Cornford (*The Origin of Attic Comedy*, London, 1934) and Gilbert Murray (*Five Stages of Greek Religion*, Oxford, 1925), examined how Greek comedy, as well as Greek tragedy, evolved from Dionysiac rites intended to invoke the spirit of fertility. The presence of the god in these rites was assured partly by a celebration of the desired result — fertile reproduction of the crops and the tribe — and partly by a triumphant excoriation of the undesirable — a driving out of hostile rivals and the spirit of famine and hard times. The resulting pattern in which invocation of festivity is followed by invective against deprivation can be found in Aristophanes and the other dramatists of Athenian Old Comedy. Some subsequent forms of comedy have stressed the festive, others the hostile element. In satire and in black comedy the hostility appears to outweigh the festivity; while Shakespearean and romantic comedy are pervaded by an air of tolerant irony.

The extreme hostility found in farce is balanced by a joyous festivity. The good life is represented by protagonists who are as carefully chosen as are the antagonists who forbid it. There can be little doubt where the chief sympathies of an audience must lie, at least for one not labouring under the same repressions as Shaw. Farce is accepted as good-humoured fun, which is most satisfying precisely when it invites violation of social taboos. There are nevertheless some farces which are so devoted to hostile joking that they seem to come close to losing their joyousness. They are farce at its most primitive dramaturgical stage, when the action is simple, straightforward and linear. The practical joke is established, pursued and its success is celebrated: that is the sum total of the piece. Only the sheer vivacity of the pranksters who represent the life-force and the obnoxious nature of the victim save this kind of farce from Shaw's charge of *Schadenfreude*; joy in the sufferings of others.

Simple pieces like this may be divided into two classes, which are distinguished by the explicitness of their aggression. 'Humiliation-farces' subject their victims to explicit degradation and celebrate their victories quite openly. 'Deception-farces', on the other hand, are somewhat more kindly. Their victims are often allowed to remain happily blind to the fact that they have been outwitted; and if not, reconciliation of some kind is sought by the practical jokers. Both kinds are essentially straightforward in their action.

The earliest independent farce in English drama, John Heywood's interlude of *John John the Husband, Tyb his Wife, and Sir John the Priest* (c. 1530), is a humiliation-farce. It was inspired by an anonymous contemporary French *farce*, the *Farce du Paste*, and the slight changes that Heywood made from his source actually increase the emphasis upon the victim's powerlessness and humiliation. Heywood introduces us to a household in which the normal social roles are inverted, with a hen-pecked husband and a loose-living wife. John John is put to work at various household tasks and bribed with the promise of a pie for supper if he will go fetch his wife's 'gossip', Sir John the priest, to share the feast. Swallowing his pride, John John agrees, but his hopes are disappointed when he returns with the guest in tow. Tyb greets him with:

> The devil take thee for thy long tarrying!
> Here is not a whit of water, by my gown,
> To wash our hands that we might sit down;
> Go and hie thee, as fast as a snail,
> And with fair water fill me this pail.

(*The Dramatic Writings*, vol. I, ed. J.S. Farmer, N.Y., 1966, p.80)

The pail has a hole, the wax for repairing the hole is hard and as John John sits chafing it at the fire, with burnt hands and smoke in his eyes, the others polish off the pie and the ale. But cowardice invites mockery and the revellers taunt the outcast mercilessly:

Sir John: What dost, John John, I thee require?
John: I chafe the wax here by the fire.
Tyb: Here is good drink, and here is a good pie.
Sir John: We fare very well, thanked be our lady.
Tyb: Look how the cuckold chafeth the wax that is hard,
    And for his life, dareth not look hitherward.   (p.83)

His pathetic asides admit the fate to which he is reduced:

John (aside): . . . . a vengeance take you both as ye sit,
    For I know well I shall not eat a bit.
    But yet, in faith, if I might eat one morsel,
    I would think the matter went very well.   (p.83)

Their jeers goad him to action at last and he flings the broken pail at his wife, demanding that the priest leave the house. Tyb urges on a noisy, but ineffectual fight (the stage direction reads, 'Here they fight by the ears a while, and then the priest and the wife go out of the place.'). But the poor husband's suffering is little altered: although he boasts of his victory in driving off the couple, he cannot escape a mental vision of their ultimate triumph:

John: . . . for by God, I fear me,
    That they be gone together, he and she,
    Unto his chamber, and perhaps she will,
    Spite of my heart, tarry there still. . . .   (p.89)

He rushes out to find further humiliation, bidding the audience a hasty good-bye.

The downtrodden husband was a standard comic butt for the late Middle Ages. Narrative *fabliaux* and dramatic farces alike made use of the triangle in which the faithless wife and the

philandering priest as the representatives of good-living op-
pose the puny and cuckolded husband, who clings desperately
to the conventional moral code. It is not so much that the husband threatens to abbreviate the lovers' gleeful pleasures, as
that he invites their scorn by his inability to deal with the situation. He can neither accept it nor amend it, since he lacks both
flexibility and determination. With some psychological vera-
city, John John carries the type to an extreme by deliberately
seeking his own martyrdom.

It is idle to deny that there is some pleasure in seeing butts of
this kind fooled to the top of their bent. Their rudimentary
motivation and their rigidity of character display more affinity
with puppet-figures like Punch and Judy than with complex
dramatic *personae*. They are the stuff of popular comedy,
which has always thriven upon the humiliation of unpleasant
villains and foolish knaves. With puppets, the fantastic nature
of their injuries is made evident. In the same way, film and tele-
vision cartoons today use caricature of outline and synchroni-
zation of movement to reassure the viewer that their creatures
will rise phoenix-like from beneath the steam-roller which has
just passed over them.

The precursors of Mr Punch and his family were the masked
actors of the *commedia dell'arte* in sixteenth-century Italy.
These also used stylized acting and acrobatic mime to convey
the distance between their acts and real-life. Communicating
primarily in such visual terms, the *commedia dell'arte* readily
adapted itself to other European countries. It was especially
popular in Vienna and Paris, where resident troupes were established during the course of the seventeenth century. Visits to
England were infrequent but well received; the inspiration of
commedia characters and their style of acting was particularly
marked after the Restoration in 1660 and can still be seen in
Harlequinades and Christmas pantomime. Punch himself
derives from the Neapolitan servant or *zanni* named Pulci-
nella. In Paris, the *commedia* actors enjoyed royal protection

until they fell into odium in 1697 by contributing to the scandal over the famous satire on Madame de Maintenon, *La Fausse Prude*. They were dismissed by the king, Louis XIV, and left Paris, not to return until summoned again by the Regent after the old king's death in 1615. Their skills had greatly influenced popular drama in Paris, from Molière to entertainments at the great urban fairs. In the early decades of the eighteenth century, these 'illegitimate' fairground theatres provided lively competition to the monopoly exercised by the official *Comédie Française*. Short introductory farces or *parades* would be played, often on a narrow stage outside the theatre, in an effort to attract patrons inside for the main burlesques and operettas. The chief characters of these *parades* were those familiar from the *commedia dell'arte*; but grown somewhat world-weary, reflecting contemporary social mores. Arlequin was the cynical valet; Léandre his elegant but dissipated master; Isabelle was the young girl, of dubious virginity; Cassandre, the aged libertine, might play Isabelle's father, or another elderly role. Various stupid clowns, modelled on the street-life of the day, provided Arlequin with a permanent butt for practical joking, and raised laughter by their antics with mistresses who were often egregiously-dressed male 'Dames'. A contemporary collection of these pieces was published in Paris in 1761 (*Théâtre des Boulevards*, 3 vols).

There were few taboos that were not broken by joking in the parade-farces. Isabelle's pregnancy gave rise to innumerable puns and situational jokes, as did the courting of the clowns. One popular piece, *Le Marchand de Merde (Théâtre des Boulevards*, vol. I, pp. 238-60) concludes with a miserable clown, Gilles, sitting forlornly in the middle of the stage with a barrel of night-soil broken over his head. Although scatalogical, this piece is by no means unstructured in its ribaldry. Gilles, having offended Léandre by careless fouling of his neighbours' doorways, is appropriately duped into believing that he can earn a professional income by marketing his own produce honestly.

Arlequin demonstrates a sale to an unsuspecting apothecary, who discovers the smelly nature of the fraud just as Gilles, staggering under the weight of his own enormous cask of merchandise, arrives to cry his wares. The clown is punished for both offences by the apothecary and is left to try and explain to his mentors that learning a trade is not as easy as it looks:

> *Arlequin*: You didn't perhaps make some mistake or other? But no; it's not a difficult profession to follow.
> *Gilles*: No really, I promise you. I didn't do anything wrong. The merchandise was good, just smell it! You'll have to bear witness to that. The rotten Apothecary, curse his arse, he just wouldn't sample it!
> *Arlequin*: It's not diarrhoetic by any chance?
> *Léandre*: We'll just have to hope, Mr Gilles, that you'll have better luck next time. Don't be discouraged and give up.
> *Gilles*: Dammit, Monsieur, I'm really fed up with this trade-business.

(Theatre des Boulevards, vol. I, my translation, pp. 257-8)

His humiliation is complete when even his intended, Catin, scornfully points out his idiocy and abandons him, still mostly uncomprehending, to brood and to take his revenge another day in another farce.

The victims of deception-farces may be no wiser than those of simple humiliation-farce, but they are certainly treated a little more kindly. The social conventions are not quite so openly violated. Cervantes' famous series of eight short *entreméses,* or interludes, provide some excellent examples of this straightforward but less vicious farce-structure. Although these pieces may never have been performed, they represent the kind of short farce that was played in between the acts of longer *comedias* in the second half of the sixteenth century in Spain. Cervantes offered them for performance towards the end of his life, when theatrical taste had changed; and finding them rejected as out of date, he published them in 1615. They are jolly pieces, whose spirit of demure festivity allows the younger generation to circumvent the older and to enjoy itself. It is enough in these farces, however, that the rebels achieve their ends, without exposing the obstacle to ridicule. Their triumph is a secret shared between themselves and the audience. while the victim remains unaware of the deception. In *El Viejo Zeloso (The Jealous Old Man*, c. 1600), Doña Lorenza and her niece Cristina are kept locked up by Lorenza's antiquated and impotent husband, Cañizares. A neighbour helpfully promises to smuggle a young man into the house, since the girls are never permitted to come out.

To the seventy-year-old Cañizares, the very word neighbour is alarming because it reminds him of an ever-present threat to his domestic peace. He explains himself to a friend:

> *Friend*: . . . But if Doña Lorenza never leaves the house and no one enters it, what are you unhappy about?
>
> *Canizares*: Because it will not be long before little Lorenza discovers what she is missing, and that will be a terrible thing — so terrible that the mere thought causes me fear, and my fear drives me to despair, and my despair embitters my life.
>
> *Friend*: I don't wonder you're apprehensive, for women like to enjoy the fruits of matrimony to the full!
>
> (*The Interludes of Cervantes*, trans. S. Griswold Morley, Princeton, N.J., 1948, p. 201)

He had good reason indeed, for, despite his presence, neighbour Hortigosa carries out her promise. She arrives offering a painted leather tapestry for sale. When the tapestry is held up to display its decoration of life-size figures of gallant knights, a real 'knight' slips into the inner room behind its cover. When their neighbour has departed with her rejected tapestry, Doña Lorenza seeks the earliest opportunity to join the intruder in the inner room, banging and locking the door behind her in a fit of temper with her jealous husband. Inside, she reports events through the door to taunt the angry old man whose suspicions fall far short of the scandal that is really being acted out:

> *Cañizares*: Lorenza, say anything you like, but never utter that word 'neighbour', I shiver when I hear it.
>
> *Lorenza*: And I quiver with love for *my* neighbour. . . . Now I'm discovering what you really are, you confounded old man; till today you had me fooled!
>
> *Cristina*: Scold her, Uncle; scold her, Uncle; she's just too shameless!   (p. 211)

Finally, she invites him to see for himself whether she is telling the truth or not. She holds open the door, but as he rushes forward, dashes a basin of water in his eyes so that the young gallant escapes unseen. The resulting squabble attracts an officer of the law, who arrives at the same time as a band of neighbouring musicians to see what the matter is. Cañizares cannot accuse Lorenza of more than having teased him and so is forced to apologize to her and to their neighbour for his unworthy suspicions. The girls' rejoicing and his humiliation are both swallowed up in the traditional song and dance which concludes every *entremés*, so that the clash between illusion and reality is never resolved. Cañizares is ridiculed precisely because he was right in suspecting the truth to have been told, and the girls have their own way while being cleared of all suspicion. The old man refuses, however, to change his mental fixation and his parting remarks to the audience have a pleasing ambivalence: 'I hope you people realize now what trials and tribulations a female neighbour got me into and you can see that I'm right in distrusting the whole caboodle of women neighbours!' He is, of course, more right than he knows. And by subscribing to his wisdom, while exploiting his folly, the farce has managed to conduct its outrageous business in the nicest manner possible, and to avoid affending the strict mores of Cervantes' time.

Perhaps a similar respect for proper social behaviour exerted its pressure on the short burlesques and farcical comedies that were played as afterpieces on the London stage of the eighteenth century. 'Deception-farce' is certainly characteristic of this period. Many afterpieces were adaptations or 'farcicalizations' of full-length comedies, often taken from the French. The comedy was broadened and made more obvious in this process, the intrigue subordinated to practical joking for its own sake, and exaggerated type-characters provided as targets for ridicule and disgrace. The actual figures of authority are defied and deceived in round-about ways, as they are in Cervantes' *entreméses*. Although the rebels intrigue with success, their victims are usually allowed to salvage the appearance of dignity.

Given such an approach, it is not surprising that current as well as contemporary opinion of that period finds it difficult to distinguish between farcical afterpieces and short comedies. A case in point is Garrick's *Miss in her Teens*. Highly popular, it was first played at Covent Garden Theatre in 1747 and was still in the repertoire and in new print at the end of the century. It was based, by the author's own admission, upon a full-length comedy by Dancourt, *La Parisienne* (1691), and Garrick was anxious to claim a more sophisticated title than farce for his short piece. But the sympathetic story of sixteen-year-old Miss Biddy and her marital prospects carries little dramatic tension to sustain the play, owing to the kindly and reasonable nature of her aunt and guardian — who is, as the maid, Tag, declares, 'a miracle; she has neither pride, envy, or ill-nature, and yet is near sixty, and a virgin.' The possibility that Aunt will force Miss Biddy into marriage against her will with an elderly suitor is discounted as a threat by the second scene of the play; and the happy reunion between Miss and the eligible choice of her heart, young Captain Loveit (alias Rhodophil), is achieved by the first scene of Act II. The rest of the play is given over to a series of rollicking scenes of farce.

First in line come the mockery and disgrace of two additional would-be suitors, a pair chosen to be acceptable as comic victims to even the most refined of audiences — types as old as farce itself, Captain Flash the cowardly braggart and Mr Fribble, the timid fop (Garrick's own role). Fribble, a lily-livered gallant of dubious masculinity, has been foolish enough to leave his quiet bachelor pursuits and venture upon the role of committed lover. Dallying with him, Biddy amply demonstrates to the audience that he lacks one essential qualification. The braggadocio Captain Flash lays competing claim to Miss and of course is eager to meet his rival face to face; or is he?

Flash: I shall soon do his business.
Biddy: As soon as you please, take your own time.
Tag: I'll fetch the gentleman to you immediately.
Flash: (*stopping her*): Stay, stay a little; what a passion I am in! — Are you sure he is in the next room? — I shall certainly tear him in pieces — I would fain murder him like a gentleman too. — Besides, this family shan't be brought into trouble on my account. — I have it — I'll watch for him in the street, and mix his blood with the puddle of the next kennel. (*Going*.)

(*Eighteenth Century Drama: Afterpieces*,
ed. R.W. Bevis, p. 99)

But Biddy and her maid Tag have laid their trap well and confront the two men with each other in a scene reminiscent of that between Viola and Sir Andrew Aguecheek in *Twelfth Night* (Act III, Sc. IV). In front of their mistress, the two men are unable to withdraw; and, since each is assured by the women that the other's bravado is a mere façade, they advance, exchange a nervous word of insult and retreat to the safety of a female escort. At length they are pushed forward, like the cardboard figures of a Toy Theatre, with swords feebly extended in fighting posture and each man ready to die of fright. It is Biddy's plan, however, to expose them both as cowards and the 'duel' is interrupted by her beloved Captain 'Rhodophil'. In uniform, he presents a perfect picture of British courage and manly devotion. The rival lovers instantly collapse and are beaten off-stage in turn. First, Flash, who is discovered to be a deserter:

> *Flash*: Nay, good Captain —
> *Captain*: No words, Sir. (*Takes his sword.*)
> *Fribble*: He's a sad scroundrel; I wish I had kicked him.
> *Captain*: The next thing I command — leave this house, change the colour of your clothes and the fierceness of your looks, appear from top to toe the wretch, the very wretch thou art; or if you put on looks that belie the native baseness of thy heart, be it where it will, this shall be the reward of thy impudence and disobedience. (*Kicks him, and he runs off.*)
> *Biddy*: Oh, my dear Rhodophil!   (pp. 101-2)

Next, Fribble the feeble:

> *Fribble*: What an infamous rascal it is! I thank you, Sir, for this favour; but I must after and cane him. (*Going, is stopped by the Captain.*)
> *Captain*: One word with you too, Sir.
> *Fribble*: With me, Sir?
> *Captain*: You need not tremble, I shan't use you roughly.
> *Fribble*: I am certain of that, Sir; but I am sadly troubled with weak nerves.
> *Captain*: Thou art of a species too despicable for correction; therefore be gone, and if I see you here again, your insignificancy shan't protect you.
> *Fribble*: I am obliged to you for your kindness; but if ever I have anything to do with intrigues again! — (*Aside, and exit.*)
> *All*: Ha, ha, ha!   (p. 102)

These easy victories however are followed by sterner stuff:

young Loveit and his Biddy have still to defy the rich but dec-
repit suitor favoured by her aunt. When the elderly Sir Simon
enters, he is shocked to discover that the formerly timid Miss
Biddy has acquired a new character: she is no longer his 'innocent moppet' and brazenly announces that she has been entertaining gallants.

> *Sir Simon*: Do you hear, Jasper? — Sure the child is
>   possessed! — Pray, Miss, what did they want here?
> *Biddy*: Me, Sir; they wanted me.
> *Sir Simon*: What did they want with you, I say?
> *Biddy*: Why, what do you want with me?
> *Sir Simon*: Do you hear, Jasper? — I am thunder-struck! I
>   can't believe my own ears!   (p.103)

Learning that Biddy's favourite gallant is still present and
willing to meet all-comers, Sir Simon finds himself trapped in
his role as would-be suitor, just as the earlier rivals were. If he
presumes to enjoy the sweets of a youthful match, he must also
earn them. Relying on his valet, he accepts the challenge, but
wishes anxiously that his son, Bob, were nearby to thrash the
upstart. Young Loveit enters and for a moment laughter
hovers on the brink of silence as the truth of the confrontation
is revealed:

> *Captain* (*approaching angrily*): What is the meaning, Sir?
>   — Ounds! tis my father, Puff, what shall I do?
> *Puff* (*drawing him by the coat*): Kennel again, Sir.
> *Sir Simon*: I am enchanted!
> *Captain*: There is no retreat, I must stand it!
> *Biddy*: What's all this?
> *Sir Simon*: Your humble servant, Captain Fire-Ball. — You
>   are welcome from the wars, noble Captain. — I did not
>   think that I should have the pleasure of being knocked o'
>   th' head or cut up alive by so fine a gentleman.   (p. 104)

Unwittingly, the rebels have stepped straight into an Oedipal situation with their practical joking and, for an instant, the joke threatens to become a serious competition between youth and age over sexual rights. But the tone of comedy, if not of farce, is preserved by an abrupt change of face on the part of the son: his swagger drops away, and is replaced with deference as he withdraws from the conflict. His father responds with a matching *volte-face* and delivers a prompt blessing on the young couple's nuptials:

> *Sir Simon*: Ay, ay, with all my heart — lookye, son, I give
> you up the girl, she's too much for me, I confess; — and
> take my word, Bob, you'll catch a Tartar.   (p. 104)

Since the rebellion of child against father has not wittingly been taken up, it can easily be laid to rest. But the festive spirit of this happy ending is enhanced by the knowledge that, in effect, the foolish lovers have stood substitutes for the father in their physical humiliation. Sir Simon receives his due share of mockery, but only when his identity is not fully understood. It is the impostors who bear the brunt of violence and ridicule. Like deception in general, this device of deflected humiliation serves to satisfy the aggressive impulses of practical jokers, while avoiding social outrage.

Such devices are put to skilful use in the Elizabethan stage-jig, *Singing Simpkin*, despite an apparent simplicity of plot. Quite possibly this piece was composed by the famous Elizabethan comic actor, Will Kemp; he certainly performed in its leading role, that of the clown Simpkin. It first appeared in London in the last decade of the sixteenth century and was so popular that it passed into the repertoire of the illegal acting troupes of the Commonwealth period. Its cheerful bawdiness, light-hearted song and dance and homely intrigue provided an appealing mixture with which to conclude the stirring performances of the Elizabethan public stages.

Jigs were made to be sung and danced to popular tunes and this one opens with the timid clown Monsieur Simpkin singing a love-duet with a lively young wife (not his own). A servant interrupts them to announce the arrival of a rowdy bully, Bluster the Roarer. Concealed in a convenient chest, Simpkin watches and comments *sotto voce* on the Wife's dealings with this new lover. Before he can be persuaded to depart, the Wife's elderly husband arrives. Quick-thinking by the Wife produces a plausible explanation which covers all aspects of the situation: she tells her husband that the Roarer has broken in to seek a mortal enemy whom he believes to be hiding in the house. The plan is endangered by the slow-wittedness of the bully, who protests that he does not suspect anyone to be hiding; but once this hitch is overcome, all goes well. Elated by her success the Wife pursues her trick one step further to explain the hidden lover as well as the obvious one:

> *Old Man* (*to* Bluster): She knows not of your enemy,
>   then get you gone were best.
> *Wife*: Peace, husband, peace, I tell you true,
>   I have hid him in the chest.
> *Old Man*: I am glad on't at my heart,
>   but doe not tell him so.
> *Wife*: I would not for a thousand pound
>   the Roarer should it know.
>   (*The Elizabethan Jig*, ed. C.R. Baskervill, p.447)

Pacified, the Roarer departs, the Old Man extricates a rather limp clown from his hiding-place and attempts to resuscitate him. But the Old Man's kindness is expended upon a farcical rogue who belies his meek and mild looks, and while the husband goes to purchase liquid refreshments, the lovers congratulate themselves on their cleverness. Their triumph is alas short-lived:

Simpkin: Thy husband being gone my love,
  Wee'l sing, wee'l dance, and laugh,
  I am sure he is a good fellow,
  and takes delight to quaff.
Wife: I'le fold thee in my arms my love,
  No matter for his listening.
  (*The Old Man and his servants listen.*)
Simpkin: Gentlemen, some forty weeks hence
  You may come to a Christning.   (p.449)

The husband's revenge is swift and to the point; the clown is beaten off stage.

The deception here clearly rebounds upon its perpetrators and the purely straightforward action of a practical joke gives way to a reverse movement. The joking is no longer unidirectional, but balanced. *Miss in her Teens* demonstrated how a moment of confrontation could checkmate the pranksters: but in that case, the young lovers were not made to suffer and the comic tone simply modulated itself as they voluntarily dropped rebellion for dutiful submission. In *Singing Simpkin* there is no change of mood: laughter continues uninterrupted by the confrontation, perhaps even heightened by it. As in the humiliation-farces discussed earlier in this chapter, the climax of the farce does not crush the victim; he simply accepts his punishment, under protest. Clown Simpkin retains enough spirit in fact to demand his promised restorative, if he cannot have his love-games:

Simpkin: But now you talk of knaverie,
  I pray where is my Sack? [sherry-wine]
Old Man: You shall want it in your Belly, Sir,
  And have it on your back. (*They beat him off.*)   (p.449)

Fundamentally, both victims and rebels respond in farce to the same realities of power. Pretensions and stupidity receive their just deserts and when conventional kill-joys such as husbands and fathers are weak figures, they invite attack. Incapacity to exploit the power which society accords encourages rebellion. The values of farce are those of *Realpolitik:* to the young and the bold goes the enjoyment of sex; to the old and the timid its frustrations; to the slow-witted, defeat is due, and to the clever, an immediate advantage. But that advantage is, like Simpkin's, temporary in nature, and when the rebels over-reach themselves, the thrust of the joke is reversed. Power remains conventionally disposed, and the rebels can win only by avoiding open warfare. To be discovered is to be caught. In this sense, Rousseau, with whom I opened this chapter, gravely misread the essential conservatism of the farcical rebellion.

3

Tit-for-tat, the world of revenge

*Georges Feydeau to Lucien Guitry, the great tragic actor,
who had asked for a Feydeau play*: 'My dear Lucien,
there are two principal figures in the comic theatre . . . he
who delivers kicks to the backside and he who receives
them. But it is never the one who gives the kicks who
creates laughter; it is the one who receives them. And
you, Lucien, you cannot receive them.'

Symmetrical patterns created by the exchange or reversal of
comic roles are in fact more common in farce than the unidirectional structures which characterize the 'humiliation-' and
'deception-farces' of the last chapter. A rebellious or mischie-
vous practical joke will often produce a counter-attack by
those whose dignity has been offended, so that the rebels are
either checkmated or suffer humiliation in their turn. This is
the structure of 'reversal-farce': a comic thrust in one direction
is reversed by a subsequent initiative in the other. In the theatre, this pattern is often referred to as 'the robber robbed'; but
probably the most familiar reversal is that already illustrated
by *Singing Simpkin*, where the wife and her lover are caught by
a returning husband, who gives the intruder a beating for his
pains.

A very crude example of this kind of reversal-farce comes
from the collection of drolls and other surreptitious entertainments of the Interregnum published in 1662 under the title *The
Wits; or Sport upon Sport* (ed. J.J. Elson, London, 1932).

Given the conditions of performance and the possibility of raids by Cromwell's soldiers, it is understandable that most of these pieces are quite primitive; *The Humour of Simple (or, Simpleton the Smith)* is no exception. This makes it however a good example of unsophisticated farce such as has always characterized fairground and street performances. Like all popular drama, it leaves room for the inspirations and exigencies of the moment and provides in its text only a situational thread upon which the beads or individual turns are to be strung, according to the improvizational skills of the actors. Even so, the overall structure is that of a simple, two-part reversal. The block-headed country bumpkin, Young Simpleton, is instructed by his father to go and court a suitable girl by 'bumfiddling' under her bedroom window. Not surprisingly, Mistress Dorothy (Doll) is unimpressed by these efforts and rewards Simpleton with the contents of a chamber-pot. This is Scene I. Scene II jumps over an unlikely marriage to show the couple seated amicably beside a domestic hearth. Young Simpleton goes off in hopes of earning some money, while Doll welcomes back two of her old sparks and indulges in fond reminiscences about old times. When they are interrupted by Young Simpleton's return, Doll suggests to the would-be lovers that they lie down by the fire and mimic a giant pair of bellows. Her husband's revenge, having enlisted the help of Old Simpleton, his father, is to treat the bellows realistically, 'working' it with insulting comments about the air-escape vent and the staleness of its wind. On this edifying note, the farce ends, with conventional authority duly restored and modish pretension punished.

Reversals need not be as arbitrary as this one, however. The joke is obviously more satisfying if the revenge proceeds logically from the initial humiliation. The anonymous French *Farce du cuvier (Farce of the Washtub*, c. 1500) is a small masterpiece in this respect. The play opens with the inversion of marital roles so common to mediaeval pieces, the wife usurping the husband's authority. Despite Jacquinot's (Johnny's) determination to escape the clutches of his wife and mother-in-law, he spends his days, like Heywood's John John, wearily helping with the housework. When he complains that the list of tasks to be performed is so long that he cannot even recall all the items, the women propose that he write up 'un rolet' (a catalogue on a scroll). He agrees, if he can bind himself to the contents of the list, no more and no less. There is a struggle of course about certain items, such as nappy-washing down at the river, and his mother-in-law has a final bright idea:

> *Mother*: Oh yes, and now and then you'll steal a moment to give her a bit of you-know-what.
> *Jacquinot*: She'll get a taste maybe once a fortnight or in a month or so.
> *Wife*: No! every day, five or six times! That's my minimum demand!
> *Jacquinot*: God save us! There's no way you'll get that! Five or six times, by St George! Five or six times: not even two or three! By God's body, no way!
>
> (*Four Farces*, ed. Barbara Bowen, Oxford, 1967, pp.24-5, my translation)

Nevertheless, the list is finally established and signed; and since it includes helping to wring out the laundry over the heating copper, Jacquinot finds himself being pressed into immediate service before the water gets too hot. But as the couple stand pulling on either side of the great vessel, an accident occurs — whether by design or chance: a great heave from Jacquinot tumbles his wife into the mess of dirty water and tangled sheets. Her pleas for help are received by one who has bound himself to a bargain, and who, search as he will, cannot find this particular command included in all the length of his scroll.

The arrival of mother-in-law is of no use either, Jacquinot simply repeats his wooden assurances to them both that the task of saving his wife's life is 'not on his list'. Finally he offers a bargain: if his wife will restore him his position as master in the house, he will relent and pull her out. She agrees ('I'll do all the housekeeping, and never ask you to help, and never order you about — except when I just have to!') and for better or worse, she is hauled out and the two are reconciled happily enough.

It is the symmetry of this construction which makes it so satisfying, and the precision with which the weapon of attack is turned back upon the attacker. The whole purpose of the agreement is of course defeated by interpreting it according to the strict letter of the law. Jacquinot has bound himself to an object — the scroll — which dominates his actions as metaphor becomes concrete; but with results that are totally unpredicted by the wife and her mother. Such a focal role for physical objects is very common in farce. Interestingly, it was a reversal of exactly this kind which Heywood preferred to omit in adapting his interlude of *John John* from the French *Farce du Pasté (Farce of the Pie)*, where the henpecked husband is driven beyond endurance by his wife and her lover until he seizes the bag of flour and literally 'makes a pie' by pasting over the Curé.

Although conventional authority is restored, mediaeval farces are not primarily symbolic fables of morality. In contrast to their sister genre, the *sottie*, in which actors masked as fools personated abstract characters, the *farces* present realistic and rather endearing human portraits. Chief dramatic interest resides in the farcical struggle for power, in which talents are well matched on both sides. If the ideal solution of a relationship of mutual love and harmony seems to be laughed out of court, these squabbles do at least conclude with a compromise. Perhaps this is the only solution possible since, from the viewpoint of farce, the rebel may well have as much logic to his claim as the legal owner. Thieving lovers do at least possess what the other men's frustrated wives desire. Court-room settings and legal trickery, like that of the famous farce *Mâitre Pierre Pathelin* (c. 1450), were in fact quite common. In the mid-fifteenth century, the leading composers and performers of farce were members of the society of young law-clerks, called the *Basoche*, which had branches throughout the country.

The quarrel for possession is tackled in a different way by Hans Sachs in *Der Rossdieb zu Fünsing (The Horse-Thief at Funsing*, 1553), one of his *Schwänke* (or 'jests') written for performance at Fastnacht or Shrovetide, when the festivities inherited from the Feast of Fools still held sway in sixteenth-century Germany. Funsing was traditionally the name of a town inhabited by credulous bumpkins. In *Der Rossdieb*, the three town elders are arguing over the most economical way to feed a condemned horse-thief until a convenient hanging-day may be set. The three, Löll, Dotsch and Fritz, come up with a perfect answer: set the thief free to fend for himself, but bind him with an oath to return on the appointed day. Naturally the thief, Ul von Frising, readily agrees to return and is even willing to leave his red cap as a pledge of good faith. But he does point out that unless he departs with a subsidy, he will have to thieve from the surrounding villagers in order to sustain himself in the interim. He exits with money in his pocket, promising the audience that he will take full advantage of these idiots. The second part of the farce shows Ul keeping his promise — that is, his promise to the audience. He has stolen various items from the three farmers and offered them for sale at market in Munchen, where, enticed by the prospect of a bargain, the farmers have fallen into his trap and purchased back their own belongings. Realizing this, the leader, Löll, proudly reveals that he has beaten the thief at his own game and pocketed some items unbought. Cries of 'thief' from the others lead to accusations of mutual dishonesty all round and the quarrel ends in a fierce and bloody fight, during which Ul creeps back on stage to redeem his other promise and his honour. Unseen, he seizes his cap but excuses himself from the gallows:

Where all are thieves, what reason then
For hanging any one for theft?
If this were done who would be left?
The thing is simple: let it pass
And drink together, glass to glass,
In Fünsing village, where, indeed,
Of gallows-tree there is no need;
But like with like, we bear life's cracks
Like honest men,
                                    So says Hans Sachs.

(*Merry Tales and Three Shrovetide Plays of Hans
Sachs*, trans. W. Laughton, London, 1910, pp.255-6)

What need indeed for gallows-tree in a town in which honest
thieves are set free by dishonest thieves who fail to see that an
honour-code can only apply to an honest man? And yet,
amongst thieves, the thief who fulfils the letter if not the spirit
of his pledge may have better title to his booty than those who
are blind to both letter and spirit.

Perhaps it is the levelling spirit of the Feast of Fools which is
reflected in a farce-structure, thus inverting the roles of fool
and wise-man, thief and honest farmer, prisoner and gaoler. In
Germany, the spirit and many of the practices of the Feast were
transferred after its suppression to the celebration of Fastnacht (Shrove Tuesday), the last day of indulgence before the
onset of Lent. It is certainly significant that Sachs' little farces
were designed for performance on that day.

The same healthy spirit of inversion and temporary indulgence was also celebrated in the Roman festival of the Saturnalia and it prevails likewise in the farces of Plautus, which
were probably played in association with that feast during the
second century B.C. The holiday spirit is exploited to the full
by Plautine sons and slaves, despite the power of the *paterfa-
milias*, who by law commanded the life and death of all members of his household, including his children. In *Mostellaria*

(*The Ghost Story*, c. 200 B.C.), the hero's father happens to be away travelling overseas and the substance of the farce is partly the high revels which take place in his absence and partly the attempt to cover them up when he unexpectedly returns. From the beginning of the play, it is clear that the scenes of drunken revelry and love-games can only continue as long as the old man is away. Tranio, the *servus callidus* (cunning slave) who is aiding and abetting his young master, rejects warnings from his honest fellow-slave, Grumio, who appeals to the gods:

> *Grumio*: Off he goes; and don't give tuppence for my warnings. Oh gods, help me. Let the master come back soon. It's three years now he's been away. Let him come home before the house and farm and everything goes to ruin. If he doesn't, there's only a few months to go before we're finished.
>
> > (*The Rope and Other Plays,* trans. E.F. Watling, Harmondsworth, 1964, pp. 28-9)

When Grumio's prayer is duly answered, the joke is to see how long it will be before the old man, Theopropides, discovers the truth.

Tranio meanwhile plots brilliantly to conceal the evidences of disorder. First, he shuts the revellers and their courtesans up inside the family house and then he spins Theopropides a cock-and-bull story about how the house was haunted and has had to be abandoned — hence the title of the play. But a moneylender seeking repayment of his loans and an elderly neighbour who knows the truth add complications, until the task becomes hopeless. When Theopropides and the old neighbour Simo make an alliance, open battle is declared between master and slave, propriety and revel. The result is a deadlock. Tranio takes refuge at the altar, refusing to admit his guilt, and infuriating his master still further. One of the revellers (now sobered up), comes to proffer help in repaying the wasted money and to beg forgiveness for Theopropides' son. This is easily achieved, but amnesty for the cheeky slave is more difficult, and it is not until Tranio points out that the punishment can merely be postponed, that a kind of reconciliation can take place:

> *Tranio*: You needn't worry, sir; I'm sure to do something wrong tomorrow; then you can punish me for both crimes at once.
>
> *Theopropides* (*after a struggle*): Ah, go on with you then. Go away. You're pardoned. (p.84)

So fundamental a balance between opposing farces, with its promise of renewed outbreaks to follow in the future — whenever holiday is once more declared — suggests a kind of technical delight in the mechanics of equilibrium. Barbara Bowen has observed this principle at work in the French mediaeval farces and she names it 'le balancier' (the counterpoise). The satisfactions for an audience in watching it operate, she suggests, do not come from an innate sense of justice so much as from 'a profound and unconscious desire to see two elements oscillate and return to equilibrium. To begin with, the first element gains ascendancy — and it is irrelevant whether this is just or not — and then the second' (*Les Caractéristiques essentielles de la farce française*, my translation, pp. 37-8). This period of licensed play clearly carries within itself the seeds of its own reversal, termination and eternal renewal.

When reversal-farce focuses narrowly upon the repeated oscillation of the counterpoise and not upon the broad sweep of a single overall reversal, it takes a shape which I shall call 'quarrel-farce'. This choreographs the progress of multiple exchanges between the quarrelling partners. There is an immense variety of ways in which the argument may be resolved in order to bring the farce to its end. One of the simplest is to present a quarrel which is essentially illusory and based upon mistaken perceptions: when the clash between illusion and reality is made plain, the farce is automatically terminated. This is also the way that many deception-farces end, except that here, instead of providing one party with a final reversal in his favour, the quarrel simply explodes and vanishes. An illusory quarrel can be structured much like a detective-novel, relying upon a master-sleuth to follow up the clues and to dispel the clouds of misunderstanding. A short and seemingly ingenuous piece like the famous *Paso Septimo* (also known as the *Paso of the Olives*) of the early Spanish dramatist Lope de Rueda (fl. 1550), illustrates just how sophisticated a joke this can become. For all his fooling, de Rueda is dealing with eternal questions about the nature of reality and perception. The old peasant Toruvio and his snappish wife Águeda nearly come to blows over the price that is to be asked by their daughter when she takes their olives to market. The quarrel is in fact absurd, since their olive-tree has only just been planted and, as the audience knows, olive-trees bear no fruit until the fifth or sixth year. Nevertheless, daughter Mencigüela is called upon to side first with one parent and then with the other. Acting as a visible counterpoise, she oscillates dutifully between the two, taking the line of least resistance:

> *Toruvio*: What do you mean, 'Two Castilian reals'? Come here, Mencigüela, how much are you going to ask?
> *Mencigüela*: Whatever you say, Father.
> *Toruvio*: Fourteen or fifteen dineros.
> *Mencigüela*: So be it, Father.
> *Águeda*: What do you mean, 'So be it, Father'? Come here, Mencigüela, how much are you going to ask?
> *Mencigüela*: Whatever you say, Mother.
> *Águeda*: Two Castilian reals.
> (*Spanish Drama*, ed. Angel Flores, N.Y., 1962, p. 16)

When blows are exchanged, it is Mencigüela who catches them all and her cries attract a friendly neighbour who offers to arbitrate the dispute. But when he calls for the olives so that he may inspect them, it has to be explained that they are not immediately at hand. Step by patient step, neighbour Aloxa tracks down the history of these elusive fruit, discovers their existence to be entirely fictitious and scolds the couple back into harmony. The girl's tears are dried and she is comforted with the promise of a new dress — when the olives are sold! Although peace has been restored, the troublesome fruit remain very real in the minds of the stubborn peasants.

Another technique for resolving the quarrel is used by Chekhov in several of his short farces. *The Bear, The Proposal* and *The Anniversary*, all subtitled 'jokes in one-act', were written for the actors of the Korsh Theatre company in the period 1885-91. Each farce dives immediately into a head-on and apparently irreconcilable clash between the opposing forces of male and female. But with profound psychological insight, Chekhov shows that a combination of attraction and repulsion is at work. Thus, although the quarrel flares up again and again, if the magnets can once be briefly aligned, they can be stabilized in mutual attraction. In *The Bear* (or *The Boor* as the title is also translated, 1888) a languishing young widow, Popova, is irritated by the arrival of a loud-voiced country-gentleman (Smirnov, the Bear) demanding payment of a debt incurred by her deceased husband. She tells him that she is fully occupied mourning her late husband and cannot concern herself with paying his debts. Such unreasonableness leads to a quarrel that becomes personal. Smirnov sees through Popova's affectation of romantic mourning and voices his cynicism about women's emotions; she responds that it is only women who are capable of faithfulness in love and that she intends to prove it by committing herself to a retreat from the world, despite the injuries to which her husband had subjected her. The Bear retorts 'You may have buried yourself alive, but you haven't forgotten to powder yourself.' The old servant Luka, who is called to eject the intruder, collapses uselessly in a faint when the Bear roars at him. But his mistress is more than equal to the situation: insults lead to a challenge and a challenge means pistols. (At this point the terrified Luka rushes out to

fetch help.) Smirnov is beginning to realize however that his
emotions are not quite straightforward:

> *Smirnov*: That's a woman for you: A woman like that I can
> understand! A real woman! Not a sour-faced nincom-
> poop but fiery, gunpowder! Fireworks! I'm even sorry to
> have to kill her!
>> (*Ten Early Plays of Chekhov*, trans. Alex Szogyi,
>> N.Y., 1965, p. 239)

And the closer the duel approaches, the more torn he becomes
until he is forced to reveal his conflicting emotions:

> *Popova* (*laughs angrily*): He likes me! He dares say that he
> likes me! (*Points to the door.*) Out!
> *Smirnov* (*loads the revolver in silence, takes cap and goes;
> at the door, stops for half a minute while they look at
> each other in silence; then he approaches Popova hesit-
> antly*): Listen . . . . Are you still angry? I'm extremely irri-
> tated, but, do you understand me, how can I express it
> . . . the fact is, that, you see, strictly speaking . . . (*he
> shouts*) Is it my fault, really, for liking you? (*grabs the
> back of a chair; chair cracks and breaks*) Why the hell do
> you have such fragile furniture! I like you! Do you under-
> stand? I . . . I'm almost in love with you!
> *Popova*: Get away from me — I hate you!
>> (pp. 240-1)

But with physical contact she discovers a matching ambivalence within herself:

> *Smirnov* (*approaching her*): How angry I am with myself!
> I'm in love like a student. . . . (*Puts his arm around her
> waist.*) I'll never forgive myself for this. . . .
> *Popova*: Get away from me! Get your hands away! I . . .
> hate you! I . . . challenge you!
> (*Prolonged kiss.*)   (p. 242)

As the servants rush in their mistress acknowledges her defeat in some embarrassment. To the surprise of the household one inflexible motivation has been converted to its opposite.

The famous early Victorian farce, *Box and Cox*, which is still occasionally revived, utilizes a similar 'flip-flop', although in this case the construction gives rise to distinctly burlesque echoes of the typical melodrama plot. *Box and Cox* was first performed at the Lyceum Theatre in 1847 and was billed by its author, John Madison Morton, as 'A Romance of Real Life'. Like other farces of that period, its claim to be drawn from 'real life' is justified to the extent that its characters come from ordinary working life — Cox the hatter and Box the printer, together with their landlady, Mrs Bouncer. But its plot is as 'romantic' and fanciful as you please. The quarrel arises when the paths of Box and Cox begin to cross in the single room which Mrs Bouncer has cunningly let to Cox by night (since he works in daylight hours) and Box by day (he works at night). When Cox is unexpectedly given the day off, a collision is inevitable. A verbal argument about rights to the room ('Your apartment? You mean *my* apartment!') becomes heated and leads to some sparring; but cowardice and the mere mention of the police quieten the two men. They agree to temporize with each other until Mrs Bouncer can get ready an additional room.

When the two begin to exchange amicable discussion however they make the discovery that both are (or have been) engaged to the same lady, a rather unpleasant proprietress of bathing machines at Margate, Penelope Ann by name. At this point, the bone of contention between them becomes something to be repudiated, not claimed (an embarrassing 'talisman', as it were), and with ironic generosity each man attempts to palm off the lady upon the other. The cry is now, 'My intended? *Your* intended!' The quarrel escalates once more, this time with a call for pistols. Discretion suggests however that dicing is a better method of resolving the affair. Since both men turn out to be using trick coins which constantly turn up heads, this merely perpetuates the deadlock. It is broken — with clear reference to the conventions of melodrama — by a letter (from Margate!) which arrives with news of Penelope Ann's timely death. When an inheritance is seen to be in question, association with the lady becomes desirable once more:

> *Cox*: And to think that I tossed up for such a woman!
>
> *Box*: When I remember that I staked such a treasure on the hazard of a die!
>
> *Cox*: I'm sure, Mr Box, you couldn't feel more if she had been your own intended.
>
> *Box*: *If* she'd been *my own* intended! She *was* my own intended.
>
> *Cox*: *Your* intended? Come, I like that! Didn't you very properly observe just now, sir, that I proposed to her first?
>
> ('*The Magistrate' and Other Nineteenth Century Plays*, ed. M.R. Booth, p. 195)

Predictably enough, a second letter arrives to set the quarrel in reverse once more: Penelope Ann has been saved from a watery death and is coming up to town. The two men fight to exit first but the pressure of time suddenly transforms their enmity and they instinctively unite in frantic efforts to barricade the door against the dreaded lady. Tense moments tick away as the action freezes. Mrs Bouncer is heard ascending the stairs; but the letter she brings is a happy release — Penelope Ann is engaged to a Mr Knox. As the rivals dance for joy, Mrs Bouncer announces that they may now separate:

> *Mrs Bouncer* (*putting her head in at the door*): The little second-floor back room is quite ready.
>
> *Cox*: I don't want it!
>
> *Box*: No more do I!
>
> *Cox*: What shall part us?
>
> *Box*: What shall tear us asunder?
>
> *Cox*: Box!

Box: Cox!(*About to embrace;* Box *stops, seizes* Cox's *hand, and looks eagerly in his face*.) You'll excuse the apparent insanity of the remark, but the more I gaze on your features, the more I'm convinced that you're my long-lost brother.

Cox: The very observation I was going to make to you!

(p. 198)

As Michael Booth has remarked in his essay, 'Early Victorian Farce' (*Essays on Nineteenth-Century British Theatre*, ed. K. Richards and P. Thomson, London, 1971, pp. 95-110), the liberal use of such melodramatic coincidences strikes a clear note of parody. But other techniques demonstrated here, which also depend upon the use of coincidence — such as the mechanical patterning of speech and counter-speech, the matching of names and attitudes, and the violent and repeated reversals in the plot — belong specifically to farce. They signal the light-hearted absurdity of all this sound and fury.

In the quarrel-farces studied so far, there has in fact been more sound than fury. Violence, where it occurs, has often been deflected to a subsidiary target — in *The Olives*, it is the daughter; in *The Bear*, the furniture takes its punishment. Where aggression has been exchanged directly between the quarrelling partners, it has been held in check by counter-forces — cowardice in *Box and Cox*; growing pangs of love in *The Bear*. The texts suggest moreover from matching verbal exchanges, from parallelism of movement and gesticulation, something of the stylization with which the farce-actors would present these quarrels on stage. All these devices ensure that the audience's interest is strategic, rather than empathetic.

One of the most violent of quarrel-farces is one written, nevertheless, in a highly naturalistic mode — a true 'drawing-room' farce. It is *Les Boulingrin (The Boulingrin Family,* 1898) by Georges Courteline (also translated as *These Cornfields!* by Eric Bentley in his 1958 volume of French farces). Here the vic-

tim is a parasite, Monsieur des Rillettes — his name means
something like 'Mr Pork-Pie' — who, intending to find a cosy
family to visit, unexpectedly intrudes upon a scene of unremit-
ting domestic strife. The charmingly furnished salon in the
Paris apartment of Monsieur and Madame Boulingrin allows
all the accoutrements of bourgeois comfort to be pressed into
service in the gathering storm of violence. The audience is fore-
warned by the maid who greets the patronizing visitor that his
expectations of a pleasant evening will be rudely disappointed.
As soon as his hosts appear, the prediction begins to be confirmed:

Mde Boulingrin: Tell me, M. des Rillettes . . . .
Des Rillettes: Madame?
M. Boulingrin (*pulling him away by the left arm*): Excuse
    me, but me first.
Mde Boulingrin (*pulling him away by the right arm*): No;
    Me!
M. Boulingrin: No!
Mde Boulingrin: Don't listen to him, M. des Rillettes. My
    husband says nothing that's worth listening to.
             (Courteline, *Théâtre*, vol. 2, my translation,
                             Paris, 1938, p.16)

The more des Rillettes tries to extricate himself from this
rude and boorish scene, the more courteously his hosts press
him to stay. But their insistent attentions only bring him dis-
comfort: competing chairs are offered him, competing cush-
ions raise his knees to the level of his eyes, competing
criticisms of the other's improprieties offend his ears. When he
politely intervenes to defend the lady, the quarrel explodes. In
Madame's absence, Monsieur illustrates the various blows,
kicks and hair-pullings that his wife inflicts upon her partner in
bed:

Boulingrin: Even, worse, sometimes in the morning, she
    whacks me with her arms, on the pretext of stretching

you what she does. (*He yawns noisily, and, miming some-
one stretching his limbs on waking, simultaneously he
hits* Des Rillettes *a resounding thwack.*) Do you think
that's pleasant? (p. 36)

Madame returns with a sample of her husband's badly corked
wine for the guest to try and Monsieur adds some soup
('genuine ratsbane', he claims). Despite firmly clenched teeth,
des Rillettes is forced to swallow some of the mixture of evil
liquids and then is drenched with the remainder, when first the
wine-glass and then the soup-plate are flung by the spouses at
each other. Worse follows: Madame pulls out a revolver and
aims at her husband, who seizes the unfortunate des Rillettes
as a shield. The lights go out and in the darkness blows (evidently received by the human shield) and insults are heard.
Then Madame fires: des Rillettes exclaims that he is hit in the
calf. A crescendo of noise and destruction ensues:

> *The voice of Boulingrin*: Ah! you're going to fire? All right,
> I shall break the mirror!
> *Voice of Madame*: Ah! you're going to break the mirror! All
> right, I shall break the clock!
> *Voice of Boulingrin*: Ah! you're going to break the clock!
> All right I shall break everything!
> (*Broken furniture rolls around.*)
> *Voice of Madame*: Ah! you're going to break everything?
> All right, I shall set it all on fire!
> (*Sound of people rushing around and shrieking.*)
> *Voice of Des Rillettes*: For God's sake be careful! You're
> treading all over me!   (p. 49)

As the fire's red light grows in intensity, a miserable des Rillettes can be seen crouched on the floor, where he is duly
drenched once again by the maid who arrives with a bucket of
water to put out the fire. In the distance, the sound of the fire-
engine arriving at full gallop is heard; and for a crowning touch
of irony, Monsieur Boulingrin appears silhouetted in the door-

way to remind his guest: 'You mustn't go, Monsieur des Rillettes! You're going to drink a glass of champagne with us!'

Courteline has traced here a psychotic escalation of the eternal marital quarrel: it moves from criticism to insults, from disguised pinchings to open blows and pistol-shots, from malicious damage of treasured objects to downright arson. Constant acceleration produces the final stroboscopic explosion of noise, light, violence and destruction. But, whether by accident or design, most of the violence is inflicted upon the intruder and, in the process, each of his expectations about the evening's visit is met with a precise reversal. He comes anticipating comfort, pleasant conversation, good food and warmth. He is tipped onto the floor, listens to scandalous abuse, is force-fed soup and wine which have been rejected as unfit for human consumption; he is hit, worried, shot at and drenched, while the comfortable hearth he seeks is converted into a raging inferno. As he remarks, 'charmante soirée!'. Yet he has no-one but himself to blame, either for coming or for staying. In this fashion, Courteline manages to marry the symmetry of a quarrel-farce to the violence of a humiliation-farce and to produce some profound observations about the psychology of human behaviour.

Other quarrel-farces achieve at least a temporary restoration of harmony — even if the fights seem destined to break out again before long. But Courteline's characters remain unchanged in any respect at a conclusion which seems to conclude nothing. The effect is positively claustrophobic, for the acceleration and the violence together create a powerful momentum, which begins to assume a life of its own. Eric Bentley points out in his essay, '*The Psychology of Farce*', that this self-contained machine also possesses 'a closed *mental* system, a world of its own, lit by its own lurid and unnatural sun' (in '*Let's Get a Divorce!' and Other Plays*, ed. E. Bentley, p.xx). He compares it to the world of the schizophrenic: it is internally consistent, but maniacal and ultimately self-destructive.

'Danger is omnipresent. One touch, we feel, and we shall be sent spinning in space' (p.xx). The power of such a world derives from the interrelation between the rigidities of character and the mechanisms of plot. This was best understood by the French philosopher, Henri Bergson (1859-1941), who, in speculating on the nature of the comic, was inspired by the plays of Courteline and other French farce-writers of his time. In the following chapter, I shall look at his theories in more detail.

4

The world of coincidence

> The vaudevilliste's art probably lies in presenting us with
> an arrangement of human events whose interior
> clockwork is evident, while at the same time it preserves
> an external appearance of probability, that is, of the
> apparent suppleness of life. (Henri Bergson, *Le Rire
> OEuvres Complètes*, my translation, Genève, 1945,
> p. 34)

Henri Bergson's monograph *Le Rire (Laughter)* proposes a definition of the comic as any instance in which 'something
mechanical is encrusted upon the living' ('du mécanique
plaqué sur du vivant', p. 35). Literary critics and psychologists
alike reject any general application of this definition and Bergson is no longer the highly regarded figure he was in his own
day. He believed that 'laughter has no greater enemy than emotion . . . it appeals purely to the intellect' (p. 17). Many critics
feel that this denies the existence of 'higher', more humane
forms of comedy, while psychologists stress the importance of
social and behavioural aspects of laughter, rather than the
mechanical structures of the comic material. In fact, Bergson
was not insensitive to these issues — indeed, he began his study
by pointing out that laughter is a social activity, the targets of
which are essentially human, commanding our sympathy in
varying degrees.

Bergson was more concerned, however, with the *forms*
taken by the comic imagination, particularly in the theatre. In

effect, *Le Rire* is a practical analysis of comic examples, drawn chiefly from farces of his day, from Moliere and from other classical French comic authors. Examining them, Bergson identified a series of mechanical devices found in situational comedy, in caricature and type-characterization, and in the structure of comic dialogue. He distinguished (pp.63-70) three basic principles of construction: repetition (of scenes, events, problems, phrases, characters, etc.); inversion (repetition with a twist or contrast; reversals and oppositions); and the 'interference of series'. This last is a term drawn from optics, which Bergson used for the misunderstandings and 'crossed-wires' which crop up with such regularity in comic dialogue and comic plot. In each case, two independent experiences intersect so that the resulting single event is interpreted in different ways by both sides. For the audience, which is privileged to see both sides of the question, the results are hilarious. The names of many minor comic patterns which Bergson identified have become standard labels of dramatic analysis and several of them will arise in the course of this chapter. All of them are based upon the operation of coincidence to produce recognizably symmetrical or mechanical structures, which will transform the free flow of dramatic action into predictable patterns.

Bergsonian effects depend as much upon a 'mechanical' approach to the presentation of character as upon mathematical patterning of events. Bergson was clearly fascinated by the psychology of caricature. He defined a type as a dramatic character who lacks flexibility and is dominated by a rigid mental set (p. 96). This inelasticity prevents the type-character from adapting properly to changes in his surrounding circumstances. Exaggeration renders him somewhat improbable; but his mental fixation produces its own internal logic, so that a comic type will behave quite consistently within his improbable world. The reverse is also true: an apparently 'normal' character can rapidly become monomaniac with the onset of farce. A type is doomed to repetitiveness both in his behaviour and in his mental processes. He is also capable of *being repeated*, i.e. of duplication. This observation of Bergson's helps to explain why like and unlike pairs of characters are so typical of farce: Box and Cox, Flash and Fribble, duplicate lovers, male opposed to female, old versus young, twins and doubles, and so forth. The artificiality of the arrangement signals both a distancing of the characters from the audience and a lessening of their humanity: they lack the flexibility and the individuality of lifm

Type-characters are moreover quite unconscious of their limitations. They act and react blindly, driven by their rigidity. Although a type is certainly capable of congratulating himself on his cleverness or his good-fortune, he will lack self-consciousness. More often than not, the audience's position of privilege permits it to foretell a downfall that is concealed from the character himself. One recalls des Rillettes' self-satisfaction at the beginning of *Les Boulingrin*, while the maid signals to the audience behind his back; or Gilles as Shit Merchant enthusiastically attempting to tout his merchandise to an already enraged apothecary. Bergson succinctly observed that the two necessary conditions for this kind of comedy are 'unsociability in the comic figure, and a lack of sensibility on the part of the spectator' ('insociabilité du personnage, insensibilite du spectateur', p.94). It follows that the audience's involvement with the actions of such characters will be more strategic than empathetic. This is not to rule out the possibility of sympathetic responses: the whole premise on which the practical joke is offered as entertainment is that the audience will enjoy watching it succeed. If no interest whatever is felt in these chattering puppets on stage, the joke will fail utterly. But to the degree that emotional self-awareness is developed by the victims and emotional responsiveness to their plight experienced by the audience, farce can and does pass on from practical joking to become a more complex form of comedy (see pp. 83-94).

One of the ways in which type-characters are barred from

exploring their own consciousness is quite simply that farce allows them no time to do so. Bergson points out that once a pattern begins to impose itself upon events in a farce, the action is forced forward to complete the symmetry. The speed and impetus of events limit the characters to helpless gesticulation, in contrast to the decisive exercise of volition permitted a fully dramatic figure. Bentley remarks that this deliberate speeding up of movement 'signifies that in farce, as in dreams, one is permitted the outrage but spared the consequence' ('The Psychology of Farce', *'Let's Get a Divorce', and Other Plays*, p. xiii).

Courteline's farce, *Les Boulingrin*, has already demonstrated how the machine which drives its plot rapidly assumes an impersonal power over all its characters. The entire cast can be drawn into the confusions and humiliations of a cosmic practical joke. When this happens, the farce assumes a circular design and works out its jokes not on the basis of revenge, but on the more alarming assumption that *no-one* is safe. Despite their complex geometrical structures, such farces can be surprisingly naturalistic on the surface. They are characteristic of the late nineteenth century and their precursor was the 'well-made play', pioneered by the prolific dramatist Eugène Scribe (1791-1861). His insistence upon a logical connection between plot and motivation encouraged the later development of naturalistic drama; and his demand for intelligible rules of construction opened the way for these highly stylized farce-structures which were triumphs of mechanical precision. Contemporary writers of *vaudeville* comedies (a genre allied to a ballard-opera, in which each scene is concluded and summed up by the singing of a *vaudeville*, or verses set to a popular contemporary tune) followed in his footsteps. With the songs omitted, and with the addition of realistic sets this is French farce as we know it today, the farce of Labiche, Courteline and Feydeau, as well as that of their English rivals, Pinero, Wilde, W.S. Gilbert and Somerset Maugham.

Among various types of circular farces there is one group whose structural principle is readily grasped. These are 'talisman-farces', whose mathematical permutations and combinations are anchored to reality by a physical object (the 'talisman'), from which all confusions flow. Usually, this is an elusive but desirable thing sought by the hero with disastrous results for the seemingly harmless characters of the play. The classic example of this type is Labiche's famous '*vaudeville-farce*', *Le Chapeau de Paille d'Italie (The Italian Straw-Hat)*. When it was first performed at the Théâtre de la Montansier in 1851, the influential critic Sarcey called it 'a revolution in *vaudeville*': the pace and style of that somewhat leisurely genre was indeed revolutionized by this fast and furious nightmare. Its popularity has proved long-lasting: it has been adapted as film (as early as 1927 by René Clair), as light opera and in many English versions (which, like most British adaptations of French farce, tend to excise the 'racier' parts).

The central situation of Labiche's farce is that his hero, Fadinard, is obliged on his wedding-day to replace a lady's hat, which his horse has inconveniently eaten. Delayed by the arrival of his wedding-party (and all his country cousins), he sets out to lead them to the Mayoral Office for the ceremony, while the lady and her fierce escort wait in his apartment for the hat. (She does not dare to return home to her husband without it.) Slipping into a milliner's on the way, Fadinard receives two unpleasant shocks: the milliner is an old flame whom he has abandoned without explanation, and the only hat of the requisite kind is owned by the Baroness of Champigny. He sets off for the house of the Baroness (wedding party in tow). A musical soiree is in progress and Fadinard is taken for the Italian tenor engaged to entertain the guests. He bargains for one of Madame's hats in exchange for the performance; but, alas, when the hat is brought, it is not the right one, *that* one has been given to Madame's god-daughter, Madame Beauperthois. Abandoning the concert and his wedding-party, who come trailing in under the mistaken apprehension that this is the wedding-supper, Fadinard is off to the new address.

He finds Monsieur Beauperthois nursing a head-cold and pondering the strange absence of his wife. Clearly this is the last person to whom Fadinard should address his request; but he is too frenzied to realize this. More and more demented in his behaviour, his manners becoming worse and worse, he now loses self-control and seizes a pair of pistols:

> *Beauperthois* (*letting go of him and shrinking away*): Murder!
> *Fadinard* (*shouting*): Don't cry out . . . or I shall be forced to commit a crime!
> *Beauperthois*: Give me those pistols!
> *Fadinard* (*beside himself*): Give me the hat! Your hat or your life!
> > (Act IV, Sc. viii, *OEuvres Completes*, vol. 3, my translation, Paris, 1960, p. 94)

Meanwhile the rag-tag and bob-tail of the wedding-party arrives, highly suspicious of these strange Parisian ways. In to M. Beauperthois' empty bedroom they trudge with tired feet, supposing this at last to be Fadinard's elegant apartment; and begin to escort the bride to bed. While Fadinard discovers his mistake and rushes home to warn the lady what has happened, his relatives are evicted by an indignant Beauperthois, who determines, for his own reasons, to find this lady and her hat.

At Fadinard's apartment, a show-down takes place. The wedding-party learn that a strange lady is inside, and they declare the marriage annulled; the lady learns that Fadinard has failed and that her angry husband is on his way. Miraculously, one of the country cousins provides an escape: his wedding present is a hat identical to the one that has been eaten! There is a final brush with the police; but when all is explained, Fadinard is declared to be a true chevalier and the hat is popped on Madame's head just as Monsieur arrives.

This circular hunt for a hat which the wedding party has been carrying with them all the time, has the effect of gradually stripping away Fadinard's facade of respectability. His true character, with all the normal sins of youth — extravagance, former lady friends and conceitedness — is exhibited before the eyes of his relatives-to-be — the very people from whom he would like to conceal it. The joke lies in the fact that they fail for so long to see the truth, despite their innate suspicion that he is trying to patronize their country-ways, and despite their righteous concern with the morals of a prospective son-in-law. Fundamentally, then, this farce is balanced in its mockery: Fadinard, for all his pretensions to grandeur, is humiliated and discomfited and the country-folk are essentially fooled by their awed reverence for all things Parisian. The farce is circular in more senses than one.

In contrast to the straw hat, a talisman may also be an object of embarrassment to the hero, who then strives to get rid of it at all costs. The contemporary farce *No Sex, Please — We're British* (1971) by A. Marriott and Alistair Foot is an excellent example of this kind of structure, which most effectively creates the sense of a worsening nightmare. The objects to be hidden mount up relentlessly, occupying more and more space and becoming heavier and heavier and more and more indestructible, until all possibility of concealment is at an end. As the title hints, the embarrassing talismans are sex-objects, ranging from pornographic postcards and blue flims to crate-loads of weighty tomes on sexual practices. The final blow is the arrival of two live call-girls — all mistakenly ordered of course (this being innocent English farce) from the Scandinavian Import Company. The guilty newly-weds, Peter and Frances, desperately attempt to prevent each new delivery. The presence of a visiting mother-in-law is not helpful; nor is the fact that she, in her own self-interest, is cultivating Peter's boss. It is a nice inversion of the normal social situation that the children are thus concerned to preserve appearances and propriety in

front of the older courting couple. But when the respectable
boss is recognized by the call-girls as a former regular cus-
tomer, truth finally is out: the representatives of propriety are
revealed to be as culpable as all the others.

When the talisman itself passes from hand to hand, tangling
the lines of communication and generally spreading confusion
between the characters, a special kind of irony is achieved. Molière used this construction in *Le Cocu Imaginaire*, a verse-
comedy which came to be the most frequently produced of his
works during his own lifetime. It was first staged in 1660, just
after its author had achieved fame with the successful première
of *Les Précieuses Ridicules* (1658). Its story revolves around
young Célie's locket, which pictures Lélie, the absent lover
whom her father has just bidden her to forget. The fortunes of
the lovers become entangled with marital conflict in the house
of Sganarelle, a blustering coward in the style of the *commedia
dell'arte*. Jealousies on both sides are inflamed when Celie
romantically faints from grief and accidentally drops the precious locket. When Sganarelle is called upon to help the young
lady, his wife observes him with this unknown female in his
arms. Having revived the lady and returned her to her father's
house, Sganarelle then comes back to find his better half examining a perfumed locket which portrays an extremely handsome youth. When Lélie himself returns from overseas,
wondering if Célie is still faithful to him, he finds the precious
locket now in Sganarelle's hands and assumes that Célie is the
wife from whom this blockhead says he has wrested the trinket.
The shock is too much for him and he too faints away, to be
resuscitated in his turn by Sganarelle's wife. Proof positive, declares Sganarelle and convinces poor Celie that this gallant is visiting his wife. Accordingly, she tells her father that she has
decided to forget Lélie and accept an alternative suitor. When
the lovers finally meet, they are so blinded by their anger and
indignation that the flow of mutual accusations continues
unhindered by illogicalities which are, of course, obvious to

the audience. The crossed lines are only further complicated by the presence of Sganarelle, who prowls around behind Lélie's back, armed to the teeth and muttering threats *sotto voce*:

Lélie: Who is your enemy, Monsieur?

Sganarelle: Who? No one.

Lélie: Then why these weapons?

Sganarelle: These? They're my protection
    Against the weather, if you've no objection.
    (*Aside.*) Now I must kill him; let me just be brave.

Lélie: What?

Sganarelle: I said nothing
    (*He punches himself in the stomach and slaps his cheeks
    to work up his anger.*) (*Aside.*) Coward, chicken, slave!

Célie: The sight of that poor creature ought to prey
    On someone's guilt; that's all I have to say

Lélie: It should indeed. I look at him and think
    In wonder of how low a girl can sink
    How she can make a mockery of love.
    (*One-Act Comedies of Molière,* trans. Albert Bermel,
                    Cleveland, Ohio, 1965, p. 88)

Not even the arrival of Sganarelle's wife forces the misunderstandings into the open. As with the quarrel in *The Olives* (see p. 51), a detached spectator is required to explode the fictions which are producing disharmony. In this case, it is Célie's maid. She begins by seizing hold of the concrete object at the root of the disagreements — the locket itself. Once its history is traced from Célie to Sganarelle, common sense can be restored; whereupon the fathers arrive, with the convenient news that the way is clear again for Lélie, since Célie's new suitor has chosen another wife. And all ends happily.

It is the characters themselves who endow Molière's locket with the power to manipulate their behaviour as if they were so many puppets on a string ('pantins à la ficelle', as Bergson termed it). If they were not so eager to believe the worst about each other, and so rigid in their adherence to that belief, the locket would remain harmless and its loss a minor event. Even so, there is little real hostility in this storm in a teacup. A talisman more dangerous in its social consequences is found in one of Scribe's numerous but underrated vaudevilles, *L'Intérieur d'un Bureau (Inside an Office*, 1823). This piece draws its laughter from the hierarchical structure of office life in a French ministry. With charming symmetry, the talisman of this vaudeville is itself a *vaudeville* — a daringly satirical song composed by young Victor (an ambitious but unreliable member of the office) at the expense of the Minister himself. Trouble begins when Victor mislays this *jeu d'esprit* and the *Chef de Bureau* discovers it being copied out — quite uncomprehendingly — by an elderly copy clerk. The clerk is sacked on the spot.

At this point however fate, in the shape of Bergson's 'interfering series', comes into play and news reaches the office of the Minister's impending dismissal. Instantly, the *vaudeville* is a document to be admired and its authorship is claimed by no less than the Divisional Head, a man whose daughter Victor would like to marry. The copy clerk — still uncomprehending — is reinstated and given a raise, when the series of events in Ministerial life intervenes once more: the Minister's resignation has been rejected and he is confirmed in power. The copy clerk is duly dismissed again and Victor rises to the occasion by bravely claiming the disgraceful document for his own. In doing so, he earns the gratitude of a future father-in-law, as well as general odium, but he is not downcast for long: the Minister — *noblesse oblige* — condescends to enjoy the *vaudeville* and its author is promoted.

These talisman-farces draw their comic force chiefly from the practical jokes played by misleading appearances upon the mind in its struggle to perceive reality correctly. At the same time, they do not overlook the practical jokes played by the body — those moments when, as Walter Kerr puts it, 'matter is undeniably master, as it is when a man is the temporary captive of hiccups' (*Tragedy and Comedy*, N.Y., 1967, p.154). The comic image central to *An Italian Straw Hat*, for example, is a sexual one: the bridegroom's eagerness to get down to business with his bride is constantly hindered by his obligation to find that tiresome hat. His wedding party's crescendo of complaints about their tired feet and empty stomachs reveals parallel frustrations on their part. All these characters are torn between social restraints of one kind or another and their bodily impulses. Sganarelle, in the traditional role of the braggart soldier, is likewise torn between a desire for honourable vengeance and physical cowardice. And Victor's anti-authoritarianism is shared (on safe occasions) even by the stuffy superiors who form the butt of the ridicule. Such comic dilemmas are a normal part of the human experience, and as such reach out beyond the circle of characters on stage to embrace the audience as well. Given the chance, we all share the same temptations and suffer the same indignities as prisoners of our bodies.

When the structure of a circular farce is not dictated by the history of a talisman, it is these moments of human weakness which motivate the plot. Bergson described the train of events they set in motion as 'une balle à la neige', a 'snowball' — a rolling ball which, from small beginnings, grows in size and speed to envelop every bystander in its final explosion and disintegration. It is a levelling device, which reveals to the audience, if not to the characters on stage, the equal culpability of all. 'Snowball-farces' often take the three-act structure described so wearily by G.B. Shaw in the passage quoted on p.21. Act I begins in quite normal surroundings of respectability, where a snowball is set rolling by a temporary aberration on the part of a leading character. Act II finds these indiscretions leading to disastrous consequences, which are offset by equal problems for many of the other characters. Act III can bring either mutual recriminations, or a shaky restoration of the façade of respectability, just in the nick of time. This 'snowball' is of course the backbone of all 'bedroom-farce'.

The farces of Sir Arthur Wing Pinero illustrate this pattern very well. *The Magistrate* (1885), *The Schoolmistress* (1886) and *Dandy Dick* (1887) all revolve around highly respectable pillars of society, whose very human desires lead them in a weak moment into regrettable behaviour. The offences of both Mr Posket, Magistrate of Mulberry Street Court, and Dr Jedd, Dean of St Marvells and unwilling host to the racehorse Dandy Dick, are so essentially mild that their discovery harms little but the sinner's ego. They serve, however, to reduce these paragons of virtue to a level more familiar to the surrounding members of their families and to the audience themselves. It is attempts to conceal the sins which are punished by most suffering. Mrs Agatha Posket's little deception about her true age, for example, leads directly to her capture in the police raid at the Hôtel des Princes (after hours) and thence to the dock in her husband's court. The magistrate's decision to rebel secretly against his wife's unreasonable instructions to stay at home leads him into the same raid and beyond in an ignominious flight through the window and across London on foot. The conclusion of the farce allows moral ascendancy to neither; but it does permit a tactical victory to the schemer who has led them all astray, Mrs Posket's young son, Cis. He suddenly realizes that he is old enough to respond directly to his instincts after all and seizes the girl he loves, despite mother's opposition:

> *Cis* (*embracing* Beattie): Hurrah! We'll be married directly.
> *Agatha*: He's an infant! I forbid it!
> *Posket*: I am his legal guardian. Gentlemen, bear witness. I
>   solemnly consent to that little wretch's marriage!
>   (Agatha *sinks into a chair as the curtain falls.*)
>   (Act III, Sc. ii, in *'The Magistrate' and other*
>   *Nineteenth-Century Plays*, ed. M.R. Booth, p.378)

As for Dr Jedd's little flutter on the races, it is a lapse which destroys the moral ascendancy of his clerical position. He is defenceless before his butler, Blore, despite the fact that the latter has lost his master's bet for him by placing it on the wrong horse:

> *The Dean*: Oh! (*To* Blore) I could have pardoned everything but this last act of disobedience. You are unworthy of the Deanery. Leave it for some ordinary household.
>
> *Blore*: If I leave the Deanery, I shall give my reasons, and then what'll folks think of you and me in our old age?
>
> *The Dean*: You wouldn't spread this tale in St Marvells?
>
> *Blore*: Not if sober, sir — but suppose grief drove me to my cups?
>
> *The Dean*: I must save you from intemperance at any cost. Remain in my service — a sad, sober and, above all, a silent man!
>
> (Act III, Sc. ii, *Dandy Dick*, London, 1959, p.77)

He is also helpless before his children, the delightfully named Salome and Sheba, who seize the opportunity to press their forbidden flirtations with the army-gentlemen to fruition.

These farce-characters of Pinero's are the reverse of irrational: their responses are dictated by a careful calculation of what the market will bear. They are not unfeeling; but between concern for others and concern for themselves, it is always self that will win out. They are, above all, human, their slips and errors those of everyman, despite the trappings of social position. J.R. Taylor points out that even their frenzies are believable. He writes:

> Once these characters exist, they are made to act according entirely to the dictates of their own natures, the only improbability permitted being that they do it with greater abandon and lack of self-consciousness than most people in real life do most of the time. They accept, that is, for the duration of the play, the logic of extreme solutions, and, having decided to act, never do things by half-measures. Hence the extraordinary situations into which they manoeuvre themselves. (*The Rise and Fall of the Well-Made Play,* p.55)

It is in the heat of these extreme measures, almost in a state of hysteria, that taboos can safely be violated without disturbing the veneer of good-breeding that is sustained by Pinero's farces. Mr Posket's revenge upon his wife is finally achieved in this way. Exhausted, dishevelled, guilt-ridden and worried about the evening clothes he is still wearing after his escape across town, he nevertheless acts instinctively and unconsciously in his role as Magistrate when he unexpectedly finds his wife before him in the dock. He is shocked to be told afterwards by his associate, Wormington, that he has sentenced her to jail:

> *Wormington*: Yes, sir — you did precisely what I suggested — took the words from me. They pleaded guilty.
> *Posket*: Guilty!
> *Wormington*: Yes, sir — and you sentenced them.
> *Posket* (*starting up*): Sentenced them! The ladies!
> *Wormington*: Yes, sir. You've given them seven days, without the option of a fine.
> (Posket *collapses into* Wormington's *arms.*)
>
> (Act III, Sc. i, p.366)

But, as his other colleague later points out, the Magistrate has only done what many husbands would long to do — perhaps what he himself was secretly longing to do: 'Oh, come now, sir, what *is* seven days! Why, many a married gentleman in your position, sir, would have been glad to have made it fourteen' (p.370).

The atmosphere of a snowball-farce rapidly becomes a bad dream for its inhabitants. In *Advice to a Player* (London, 1957), Denys Blakelock writes that the experiences of Mr Posket and Dr Jedd were only too real to him when he played the parts on stage. Georges Feydeau, however, was responsible for heaping far worse tortures upon his heroes and heroines than did Pinero. The cosily domesticated Parisian husbands and wives of the world of Feydeau day-dream more dangerously than their respectable English counterparts; and not surprisingly they suffer accordingly more. Two of Feydeau's mature works which are both familiar to English audiences from revivals in recent years are *L'Hôtel du Libre-Echange (Free-Change Hotel*, 1894), which has also been adapted by Peter Glenville as *Hotel Paradiso* (1957), and *La Puce à l'oreille (A Flea in her Ear*, 1907). In both plays, dissatisfied spouses set out to a 'hotel of assignation' to seek revenge on their marriage-partner. What happens at the hotels is a dreadful sequence of terror, violence, and claustrophobia. Whichever way the victims turn, whichever room they plunge into, whichever staircase they take, the very persons they should not meet appear before them, cutting off escape. According to a contemporary of Feydeau, the dramatist's rule was to throw together as soon as possible the very characters who must under no circumstances meet each other. In a snow-ball farce, the result is a series of explosions of laughter.

Innocent and guilty suffer alike in these snowballs; a fact which has led some critics to insist upon the element of cruelty in Feydeau's comedy. In a production, however, and in the actual heat of the moment, the audience is allowed no time for compassion. When, in *La Puce à l'oreille*, Raymonde takes it into her head to trap her husband, Victor-Emmanuel, by making a secret assignation with him at the Hôtel du Galant-Minet (the Hotel of the 'Galant Pussy-Cat'), she is surprised to find her own lover (supposedly no more than a platonic one) waiting for her hidden under the bed-clothes. The reason is that the modest Victor-Emmanuel has concluded that it must surely be his handsome friend to whom love-letters are being addressed, and not himself. Not only is Raymonde's plot thus thwarted, but her friend, being a warm-blooded man, reacts as circumstances invite at finding himself and his darling alone in a hotel room. And escaping from one rape, Raymonde is caught up in the hotel's famous revolving bed which swings her into the path of another, this time at the hands of the clumsy English satyr, Mr Rugby. (This character understandably became Bavarian for the English stage.) Escaping again, Raymonde encounters the hotel porter, her husband's double. Not until both she and her lover have gone on their knees to this surprised figure and extracted kisses of reconciliation and forgiveness, do they learn that there may be some mistake. Thenceforward, one member of the household after another arrives at the hotel, creating threats of recognition and disgrace which culminate in pistol-shots, door-splintering and a general outcry attracting the police.

In the midst of all this, Raymonde's husband has indeed arrived at the hotel — for the best of motives — and is surprised to find so many of his acquaintances there. But he is even more surprised to find himself attacked by the fierce proprietor of the hotel, who accuses him of neglecting his duties and kicks him off stage to don his porter's uniform. Between attempts to humour this lunatic inn-keeper and attempts to follow his wife, whom *he* recognizes, although she also treats him as a porter, the atmosphere of a bad dream becomes a little too realistic for poor Victor-Emmanuel's comfort, and perhaps for his sanity.

The marriages of Raymonde and her friends are not really threatened by the flirtations and suspicions in which the various partners indulge. The couples of *L'Hôtel du Libre-Echange* are far more culpable, by normal social standards. The middle-aged Angélique is a ferocious tyrant who domineers over her little builder-husband, M. Pinglet. Their neighbour, M. Paillardin the architect, who is also Pinglet's business partner, is quite useless for his wife's purposes. He is, moreover, callous enough to ignore her complaints. Greatly daring, Pinglet proposes to Madame Marcelle Paillardin that they supply each other with the means of revenge one evening at the Hôtel du Libre-Echange.

Their efforts are dogged by misfortune, however: the hotel turns out to be rather seedy, the porter sneers and Pinglet's amorous advances are constantly interrupted:

> *Marcelle* (*disengaging herself*): I can't understand what's come over you! I've never seen you like this before! Really! Pinglet! Monsieur ... Benoît! The champagne must be going to your head!
>
> *Pinglet*: Ah, I can't tell what it is that's going to my head! It's you! It's dinner! the wines! the liqueurs! this cigar! Ah, my wife is always telling me that I can't smoke, that I can't drink wine, that it will make me sick! Oh yes, look at me — am I sick? I want you, I want you! (*He sits down, holding* Marcelle *in his arms; the chair breaks*.) On no! Oh, damn and blast it!
>
> *Marcelle* (*bursting into laughter*): Oh, you look so funny like that!
>
> (Act II, Sc. vi, *Théâtre Complet*, vol. IV,
> my translation, Paris, 1950, p. 73)

Madame Pinglet's suspicions prove justified in fact:

> *Marcelle*: What's wrong?
>
> *Pinglet*: I don't know! I feel a chill mounting to my head! It must be emotion — it's nothing! (*Passionately, taking her in his arms*.) Ah, Marcelle! Here we are now alone, tête-a-tête! I wish you could see what's happening inside me! I feel my heart ... my heart ... Oh, lord — my heart is turning over!
>
> (Act II, Sc. vi, p. 74)

He exits hurriedly in search of fresh air and things go from bad to worse. Marcelle, preparing tea to revive him, encounters a family of her acquaintance also staying in the hotel and, as in a dream, finds herself conducting a tea-party when her would-be lover returns. Her husband appears on the scene (investigating a report of hauntings at the hotel, during which process he is thoroughly terrified), and the usual snowball leads to a comic explosion and a police-raid in which the sinners are led away to the police commisariat.

In the meantime, Madame Pinglet the tyrant has also been suffering disasters; and the next morning she arrives home with a black eye and an unlikely story about a run-away horse and an overthrown carriage. Chance plays into her husband's guilty hands when a police summons is delivered incorrectly issued to 'Madame Pinglet and Monsieur Paillardin, taken last night at the Hotel du Libre-Echange'. Now the tyrant cowers before her wrathful husband. But the situation is untenable and all the parties concerned eagerly seize the first opportunity which presents itself to shuffle off the blame to yet another pair of visitors to the hotel from the Pinglet establishment — Victoire, the maid and young Max, the student. Punishment brings its own reward for these two, as it did for young Victor in *L'Intérieur d'un bureau*, when the Commissaire de Police returns to Max, as the supposedly guilty party, the substantial bail deposited by his elders. This is the price which those who dared dream of adultery and revenge must pay to save their reputations, even if their dreams were never consummated.

The targets of Feydeau's jokes were not confined to the respectable bourgeoisie. Many of his farces deal with the brilliant world of the Belle Epoque, where young men of means were accustomed to provide an establishment for a mistress certainly before marriage and often afterwards as well. His most famous farce, *La Dame de chez Maxim (The Lady from Maxim's*, 1899) propels a rather risqué lady from this world into direct collision with the solid virtues of a bourgeois household, much to the confusion of its master. Other farces, such as *Un Fil à la patte (One String in the Hand*, 1894) and *Occupe-toi d'Amélie! (Keep an Eye on Amelia!* 1908, adapted in 1959 by Noel Coward as *Look after Lulu*) depend upon an ironic inversion of values for their comic rebellions and revenges: the very ladies who are so free and easy with their favours display a strange possessiveness about their lovers. But love, fidelity and suchlike aspirations of the spirit are no more than a joke in farce. Marriage and mistresses alike are undertaken for convenience, the one for money, the other for sex. If it is unthinkable that a man should marry his mistress, even worse is the fate that befalls the devious hero of *Occupe-toi d'Amélie!*, Marcel, who finds himself married to his *friend's* mistress, in punishment for not keeping a good enough eye upon her during the friend's absence. The ladies themselves share these practical attitudes: marriage is a triumph, but failing that, power over a lover will do, and with it, money. Amelie, for example, when presented with visiting Royalty as a client, willingly circumvents her jealous lover to gain time for an audience or two. The possessive Lucette, heroine of *Un Fil à la patte*, is equally anxious not to offend her wealthy Spanish General while she contrives at the same time to disrupt her lover's engagement-ceremony.

Between the demands of these '*cocottes*' ('chicks'), and romantic attachments to married ladies, as well as actual wives or fiancees, Feydeau's libertines in fact possess little liberty. The battle of the sexes in farce revolves around the two poles of security and freedom and in the end it is unclear which one is preferable. Is a wife more galling than a constant mistress? Is a jealous lover more troublesome than a dictatorial husband? Is the social glamour of being a 'cocotte' worth the trouble of unwanted admirers? Is a lover more convenient to the husband or the wife? Furthermore, after the introduction of divorce in France in 1883, marriage itself no longer needed to be seen as irreversible, at least in cases of adultery. This legal loophole gives rise to further comic possibilities, such as the ironic inversions in Sardou's famous *Divorçons! (Let's Get a Divorce!* 1880). Here, once divorce is agreed to, the romantic lover loses his advantages to the liberated husband, who, with consummate skill, recaptures his wife beneath the outraged lover's nose. An arranged divorce similarly offers Marcel in *Occupe-toi d'Amelie!* both escape from his arranged marriage and revenge upon his friend, who provides the subject to be discovered *in flagrante delicto*.

The force which impels all these characters of Parisian farce is, of course, the human appetite for sex and its demand for satisfaction. As openly as Feydeau and Labiche were able to approach this subject, the farces of the *commedia dell'arte* outdo them in exploiting it. K.M. Lea in her study *Italian Popular Comedy* describes how the treatment of love characterizes the gradual transition of *commedia* plots from classical romance to farce; how the love-interest passes from sympathetic young lovers (the *innamorati*) to the ridiculous affairs of the old men (the *vechii*, who are both fathers and husbands like Pantalone and Coviello), and from thence to the *zannis*, or clowns themselves, until what is at stake is not love-interest but the universal sex-drive. One of the scenarii collected by Lea in volume II of her study presents this all-embracing joke in a completely circular pattern of ironic reversals. This is *Li Tre Becchi (The Three Cuckolds*, c. 1620), which has been made familiar to readers by a rendition in volume I of Eric Bentley's *The Classic Theatre*. It should be noted that this version does more than merely flesh out the bare bones of the scenario with dialogue; it also distorts the symmetry of the original with additions and omissions.

In the original *Three Cuckolds*, three households of married couples are lined up on stage. From house Number One, jealous old Coviello and his pretty young wife Cintia appear, squabbling as usual. When Cintia goes in, Coviello confides to the audience that his neighbour's wife will be more sympathetic. He knocks at the door of house Number Two, where Pantalone the old miser lives with his elegant wife, Flaminia. Flaminia arranges to trick her husband into admitting Coviello to the house concealed in a huge chest of lemons (explanations of why a chest of lemons are left for the actor to improvize). Pantalone reveals in Flaminia's absence that he finds his neighbour Zanni's wife Franceschina more comfortable than his own; and over at house Number Three he arranges with Franceschina to visit her after he has delivered the lemons. The circle is completed when a young stranger, Leandro, arrives to renew acquaintance with the unattached wife, Cintia, in house Number One.

Round two of this charade concerns the 'rites of passage', as each lover in turn plays out his entry-trick. Zanni, who is too stupid to have a second door of his own, helps Coviello into his chest and gloats over the joke being played on rich old Pantalone. But as he stands alone on stage congratulating himself on Franceschina's honesty, *all* three houses emit contented sounds as the lovers fall into bed.

Round three progresses to the problems of a safe escape. Zanni, standing at his own front door, is bribed with the promise of a tart (Lea's plausible suggestion for what the scenario refers to as the '*lazzi* of the tart', or 'the tart-trick') to keep his eyes closed while an exhausted Pantalone staggers out to safety. Over at house Number Two, Flaminia tells the old man a superstitious tale to make *him* hide his eyes while Coviello hurriedly exits. Coviello finds his own wife innocently giving a bowl of soup to a poor beggar — Leandro in disguise. After Leandro is driven off, unrecognized, Zanni encounters him and the two exchange stories of Coviello's trick on Pantalone and how Coviello himself has been punished by Leandro. When Pantalone re-enters, Zanni and he share the joke on Coviello and to cap it, Pantalone maliciously tells Zanni how much more cleverly he has been fooled. Zanni takes his revenge by revealing to Pantalone what Coviello has been up to. When Pantalone and Coviello come face to face, they can only shriek 'cuckold' at each other in impotent fury.

The permutations of the plot are not yet exhausted and in true *commedia* style, the masked characters return for an encore, the actors determined to exact revenge upon each other by seeking new assignations. Using a traditional *burla* ('joke'), Pantalone is clapped into a basket of dirty laundry to be carried into Zanni's house and frightened with threats of being thrown into the boiling copper. He finally makes a safe entry. Coviello revisits Flaminia and Leandro takes advantage of his absence to slip in to see Cintia once more. But Zanni's suspicions have been raised in the by-play with the laundry and he returns to find the door locked against him and enough suggestive noises from within to arouse his fury. His outcry and threats to burn down the house arouse everybody and each door produces its quota of guilty lovers to meet in a grand confrontation. Now, each husband is forced to the realization that his revenge has only facilitated his neighbour's revenges and that all insults are useless. To conclude, the scenario indicates that Leandro as the odd-man-out explains 'what each has done to the other and delivers over to each his proper wife with whom he is content at last. They go in and the comedy ends' (Lea, *Italian Popular Comedy,* vol. II, p. 582).

It is not difficult to recognize the delights of the same symmetry in the highly successful one-act farce by Tom Stoppard, *Dirty Linen* (1976). The title evokes at once a farcical landscape in which familiar characters deal with the unpleasant realities of human existence: Jacquinot and his wife rinsing bed-sheets in the copper; old Pantalone and his worthy successor, Sir John Falstaff, in *The Merry Wives of Windsor*, Act III, Sc. iii, stuffed half-naked into dirty laundry; and Feydeau's hotel proprietors counting their soiled linen. Here it is a parliamentary Committee on Moral Standards in Public Life which, with some reluctance, is conducting its inquiry into that same dirty linen, in the shape of allegations of impropriety in high places. The reasons for reluctance rapidly become clear from the members' relations with the committee secretary, Miss Maddie Gotobed, a shapely red-head whose knowledge of short-hand is suspiciously slim. Their behaviour, beginning with the Tweedledee-and-Tweedledum-like pair of Conservatives, Cocklebury-Smythe and McTeazle, is a mixture of public formality and private preoccupation with French lace panties, French restaurants and French phraseology. When all the other committee members, regardless of political party or sex, follow suit, the circular nature of the joke becomes clear: the committee has met not to investigate but to conceal the truth of the rumour that some young lady singlehandedly is 'going through the ranks like a lawnmower in knickers', as McTeazle puts it (*Dirty Linen and New-Found-Land*, London, 1976, p. 15); and that young lady is Maddie.

Despite the attractiveness of Stoppard's characters, there is never any question of serious romance in these relationships. The very scale of events signals absurdity — McTeazle reports that Maddie's list of conquests, according to the *Guardian*, has reached 'at a Conservative estimate sixty-three Members of Parliament, and at a Labour estimate one hundred and fourteen' (p.29). Stoppard is dealing with the levelling joke of the inexorable male response to a pretty girl and, *mutatis mutandis* as Cocklebury-Smythe would say, with hers to the challenge of a whole pool of untapped male talent. As the committee meeting proceeds, the spirit of conspiracy among the members intensifies until they are all united against a lone, Puritanical late-comer, ironically named French. With some help from Maddie, he explodes the cover-up; but, in the process of exposing his colleagues, he himself falls victim to Maddie's charms and the committee is able to vote unanimously to close its investigation. 'Toujours l'amour', admits French, as he wipes his brow with a pair of French lace panties (p.75).

The motives of Miss Maddie Gotobed remain ambiguous, even at the conclusion of the farce. It is she who dictates the final wording of the committee's resolution, which is a victory for common sense over the conventional obfuscations which pass for parliamentary procedures. But she deliberately raises more fundamental issues still with her practical stand of defiant innocence. Does private morality really have anything to do with the conduct of public office, she asks; or, if it does, should not those watchdogs of democracy, the press, have their morals investigated likewise? People, she claims, 'don't care what M.P.s do in their spare time, they just want them to do their jobs properly, bringing down prices and everything' (p.32). To the departing backs of the committee she shouts 'I wouldn't have bothered if I'd known it was supposed to be a secret — who needs it?' What after all is the point of breaking all records if you can't boast about it? But she continues 'I sometimes wonder if it's worthwhile trying to teach people' (p.53). Beyond this nice reversal of normal sexual conventions of dominance and discretion lies a denial by the taboo-breaker that any taboos have been violated. If the joking becomes educational for its victims, then as Maddie remarks in conclusion of the play, 'Finita la Commedia' ('the comedy is over') (p.75).

Juxtaposed to *Dirty Linen* is the episode of a naturalization case — the 'American connection' as Stoppard calls it — *New-Found-Land*. Here the satirical shadow cast upon the doings of Westminster and Whitehall is deepened by the fact that the case is resolved, not on its merits, but because the Home Secretary also is compromised by the presence of Maddie and her committee. The topicality of both plays, in a year of Washington sex scandals and American deportations, together with the dramatist's acknowledged personal interest in the naturalization case at issue, encourages the audience to reflect as well as to laugh. Perhaps *Dirty Linen* is a farce on the point of becoming something more serious. I shall look at this borderline area in more detail in the next chapter.

5

On the borderline

> Farce can so easily become a tragedy. What in one
> moment can produce irresistible laughter can in the next
> produce poignant grief. There, briefly, you have the
> difference between farce in real-life and farce in make-
> believe. And we in the theatre are constantly on the qui
> vive for the humorous side of every situation. (Tom
> Walls, noted farce-actor at the Aldwych Theatre, in his
> Foreword to H. Simpson, *Excursions in Farce*, London,
> 1930)

It is worth recalling at this stage what kind of joking is characteristic of farce. Firstly, it invites laughter by the violation of
social taboos, whether those of adult propriety, or those of hier-
archy. It nevertheless avoids giving offence (which would dim-
inish the laughter), usually by adhering to a balanced structure
in which the characters and values under attack are ultimately
restored to their conventional positions. Structural stylization
and mechanical patterning also help to distinguish the festive
licence under which these attacks are carried out. The aggression is both sufficiently precise to be psychologically valid and
yet sufficiently delimited to qualify as play. Secondly, these
jokes are not designed primarily as dramatic vehicles for satirical comment upon the way of the world. Their spirit tends
rather to an indulgent, perhaps an ironic acceptance of the
human condition. Thirdly, the participants in the joking are
not usually self-aware characters who reflect upon their mis-
chief and its consequences. They are type-characters whose

automatism is obvious and whose playful plight demands little sympathy, whether they are the first or the last victim of the round. Essentially, the comic spirit of farce is one which delights in taboo-violation, but which avoids implied moral comment or social criticism, and which tends to debar empathy for its victims.

In the course of this survey, *Dirty Linen* has not been the first farce which began to escape these bounds, but is the first to do so in the dimension of a serious or satirical purpose. Satire does not require empathetic figures for its provocative statements about a corrupt or absurd state of affairs, indeed if it does involve them, perhaps it risks falling into what James L. Smith has called 'the melodrama of protest' (*Melodrama*, London, 1973, pp.72-7). In *Dirty Linen*, although the justice of Maddie's cause is easily granted — since it stands for honesty as against evasion — it is difficult to find her truly sympathetic. Certainly she is good-humoured, until the men exasperate her with their locker-room fantasies about dining at the Coq d'Or Restaurant. But ultimately the war she wages is a power-play and she remains detached and a little impersonal even in her triumph.

The protagonists of Oscar Wilde's *The Importance of Being Earnest* (1895) are similarly unemotional in their battles. It is a commonplace of criticism to observe that Wilde's characters are so monstrously egocentric as to banish sentiment and romance from the scope of the play. The battle of the sexes here takes place in a world which lacks an emotional dimension, where every move is calculated and choreographed in advance. Such detachment, allied to what Leo Hughes calls the dramatist's 'wholly-abandoned and delightful pursuit of the improbable' (*A Century of English Farce*, p. 49), tempts one to think of the play as farce. But Wilde is determined to point out common sense with his nonsense; and his highly-wrought wit acquires the force of satire. Contemporary Victorian society stands indicted for having rendered love-making a purely rational affair of business, and social respectability more a matter of luck than good-management. It is impossible to ignore the ridicule underlying the laughter of barbs like the following from Lady Bracknell to Jack, as a would-be suitor:

> *Lady Bracknell*: I have always been of the opinion that a man who desires to get married should know either everything or nothing. Which do you know?
>
> *Jack (after some hesitation)*: I know nothing, Lady Bracknell.
>
> *Lady Bracknell*: I am pleased to hear it. I do not approve of anything that tampers with natural ignorance. Ignorance is like a delicate exotic fruit; touch it and the bloom is gone. The whole theory of modern education is radically unsound. Fortunately in England, at any rate, education produces no effect whatsoever. If it did, it would prove a serious danger to the upper classes, and probably lead to acts of violence in Grosvenor Square.
>
> (Act I, *Plays*, Harmondsworth, 1954, p.266)

When the actors of farce demand our sympathy, an even more decided shift in tone takes place. J.L. Styan remarks in his study *Drama, Stage and Audience* (Cambridge University Press, 1975) that 'in any analysis, the quality of comic style, and thus its meaning, rests finally upon the comic actor' (p. 87). The dramatic event is in his hands to be moulded into this or that form, depending upon the interpretation he chooses to give it. Perhaps it is in recognition of this fact that the French word *farceur* connotes the actor as well as the playwright, both creators of farce. In any case, the central image of farce, as we have seen, possesses an especial ambivalence which can be powerfully exploited by a fine actor. In celebrating its festive licence to indulge our natural impulses, farce must equally celebrate their tyrannous rule. In the face of irresistible forces — the mechanical demands of the body, the mechanical patterns of habit, the universal laws of mechanics themselves, and beyond all these, the mechanical manipulations of the plot — farce acknowledges our common helplessness.

It follows that the mask of the farceur has two faces: the actor may present the joke of his licensed aggression or the joke of his ultimate submission. Colley Cibber recalled in his *Apology for the Life of Mr Colley Cibber, Comedian* (London, 1740) how the famous farce-actor James Nokes (d. 1696) exploited this duality in a moment of comic terror, when he 'sunk into such a mixture of piteous Pusillanimity, and a Consternation so ruefully ridiculous and inconsolable, that when he had shook you, to a Fatigue of Laughter, it became a moot point, whether you ought not to have pity'd him' (*An Apology*, ed. B.R.S. Fone, Ann Arbor, Michigan, 1968, p.84). Evidently, Nokes achieved a farcical *tour de force*: that full roar of laughter, tinged with recognition of a common humanity, which marks the high points of the genre.

For many critics, empathy is the means by which farce redeems itself and becomes significant — becomes comedy, in fact. L.J. Potts pronounces in *Comedy* (London, 1948) that 'farce is comedy with the meaning left out; which is as much as to say, with the comedy left out' (p.151). More exactly, farce is comedy with *self-awareness* left out. If Nokes were to have paused long enough to have acknowledged his folly to himself and to the audience, and to have criticized his compulsive behaviour accordingly, the farcical tone of his performance would have changed. At the very end of Chekhov's little masterpiece, *The Bear*, for example, there is a pause which allows the actors to adjust their masks in this way. When the terrified servants return to defend their mistress, they find the duel abandoned in favour of a prolonged embrace, and the action freezes. The pressure on the leading actors is unmistakable and, in some embarrassment, Popova extracts herself from the kiss, unable to meet the astonished eyes of her servants — or those of the audience. Instead, she countermands the order she gave at the beginning of the play for extra oats for her former husband's favourite horse:

> *Popova (lowering her eyes)*: Luka, tell them in the stable not
> to give Toby any oats today.
>   CURTAIN   (p. 242)

Humanity has entered the realm of farce.

In the world of the silent film, Chaplin made this mixture of farce and humane pathos peculiarly his own. *City Lights* (1931) offers a good example. Sitting alone with the blind girl who believes him to be a wealthy man, Charlie is discussing the possibility of a cure for her blindness, while he helps her wind a skein of wool. Suddenly, he shifts uncomfortably: she has begun to wind a loose thread from his underwear. Rather than distress her, Charlie accommodates its progress with great delicacy, and layer by layer he is stripped from top to bottom beneath his baggy outer garments. While we are laughing, a subtitle informs us that a Viennese doctor can cure blindness and the girl exclaims excitedly 'Wonderful! Then I'll be able to see again!' The tramp/millioniare who has offered to help the girl he loves looks directly at the camera, alarmed, threatened; and for a second we realize that, despite his comic squirmings, there will be no happy ending for the benefactor, even if there is one for her.

Such admissions of humanity on the part of the actors in farce tend ultimately to discredit the aggressiveness of their joking. The comic tone softens. Festivity itself becomes more muted, the improprieties less outrageous and, as *Miss in her Teens* demonstrated, the rebels resign themselves to an appeal for forgiveness. Having been invited to share the actors' perspective, the audience begins to share in their fortunes and can no longer follow the strategic patterns of joke and counter-joke with detachment. It begins to matter, for example, whether a match is really a love-match and not just a physical match; whether the parents and guardians are reasonably reconciled to the festive ending; and most importantly, whether any feelings have really been hurt. Chaplin, the target of much violent joking himself, never risks losing our sympathy by perpetrating violence on others.

In 1772, Oliver Goldsmith attacked the prevailing taste for sentimental comedy with his *Essay on the Theatre; or A Comparison between the Laughing and Sentimental Comedy. She Stoops to Conquer*, acted at Covent Garden in 1773, was a highly successful part of his attempt to restore the 'laughing' tradition. But the play itself, for all its practical joking and deceptions, is not farce. Its comic spirit insists upon the interplay between the true feelings of its characters and the masks they choose to wear. When Miss Hardcastle begs permission to continue in her role as barmaid in order to test her lover, Marlow, her father reluctantly responds: 'Well, an hour let it be, then. But I'll have no trifling with your father. All fair and open, do you mind me?' Poor Marlow, his illusions that he is staying at an inn rudely shattered, rounds on his friends with 'So, I have been finely used here among you. Rendered contemptible, driven into ill manners, despised, insulted, laughed at'; and though *we* may not treat him with full seriousness, his friends do. Even young Squire Lumpkin, lout that he is, demands attention for his point of view. In Act V, when the gentry from London first blame and then bless him, he retorts with spirit: 'Ay, now it's dear friend, noble Squire. Just now it was all idiot, cub, and run me through the guts. Damn your way of fighting, I say. After we take a knock in this part of the country, we kiss and be friends. But if you had run me through the guts, then I should be dead, and you might go kiss the hangman.' And Marlow's friend Hastings replies, 'The rebuke is just' (*Selected Works*, Harvard U.P., 1951, p.819).

When each character is allowed to claim attention for his point of view like this, the butt of the practical joking is capable of creating a particularly awkward pause in the laughter. Later in Act V of *She Stoops*, after Mrs Hardcastle has been led a dreadful dance by her lively son she makes a strong bid for her right to respect. Goldsmith counters this with a shamelessness and a logic which effectively preserve the comedy:

> *Mrs Hardcastle*: Yes, I shall remember the horse-pond as long as I live; I have caught my death in it. (*to* Tony) And is it to you, you graceless varlet, I owe all this? I'll teach you to abuse your mother, I will.
>
> *Tony*: Ecod, mother, all the parish says you have spoiled me, and so you may take the fruits on't.
>
> *Mrs Hardcastle*: I'll spoil you, I will.
>
> (*Follows him off stage. Exit.*)
>
> *Mr Hardcastle*: There's morality, however, in his reply.
>
> (p.822)

The case of Malvolio in *Twelfth Night* is not so easily resolved. Any audience will readily grant that the plot against him is a delightfully entertaining practical joke in the best spirit of farce; although some critics have found pathos in the scene in which Feste the clown, pretending to be a priest, visits the madman in his confinement (IV, ii). Certainly, it is in this scene that the comic tone begins to waver. The conspirators themselves voice doubts about the consequences of their joking. Sir Toby sends Feste back to revisit Malvolio 'in thine own voice', muttering 'I would we were well rid of this knavery. If he may conveniently be delivered, I would he were, for I am now so far in offence with my niece that I cannot pursue with any safety this sport to the upshot' (IV, ii, 68-73). When the Lady Olivia herself takes his part, Malvolio's parting shot — 'I'll be revenged on the whole pack of you!' — is imbued with a certain seriousness. Depending on the choices made by actor and director, this will perhaps not be enough to outweigh the comedy's overall spirit of festivity, as some critics have felt. But it is enough to illustrate my point that farce risks its immunity when its jokes become shame-faced about their aggressions.

Whenever a true love-match is at issue, the ultimate disposal of the obstructive victim will present a similar problem. This

commonly occurs in English farces which tend toward sentiment, like Brandon Thomas's famous piece, *Charley's Aunt*
(1892), for example. Here the obnoxious victim of Charley's
supposed aunt is a repressive guardian, Mr Spettigue, who con-
trols the destinies of two out of the three eligible young ladies
in the play — Miss Amy Spettigue and Miss Kitty Verdun.
Two Oxford undergraduates, Jack Chesney and Charley
Wykeham, have persuaded their talented friend, Lord Fancourt Babberly to impersonate the missing aunt, Donna Lucia
from Brazil, so that the girls will agree to be entertained at
lunch. Complications arise however when both Jack's sympathetic father and the unwelcome Mr Spettigue join the party
with the intention of courting the rich Donna Lucia. Despite
the boys' qualms of conscience and the unexpected arrival of
the real aunt, the three of them manage to extract from Mr
Spettigue all that is necessary to clinch both engagements. The
price is 'Donna Lucia's' promise of marriage. Thus at the final
unmasking, it is the guardian who suffers most, not the impos-
tor Aunt, since girls and wealthy match alike have slipped from
his grasp. Insult is added to injury by the fact that the *real*
Donna Lucia has been won by Jack's father, also a convenient
widower.

Following Shakespeare's example, Thomas provides an
angry exit for the irate victim:

> *Spettigue*: You will pardon me if I retire. (*Goes below otto-
> man to door, right. Turning to* Lord Fancourt.) As for
> you, sir, I shall inquire from the authorities, your college
> — in the morning.
>
> (Charley's Aunt, London, n.d., p.97)

Meanwhile, the necessary gestures of sympathy and remorse
are made by the other characters:

> *Amy* (*up centre, coming forward — indignantly to* Char-
> ley): Charley (*Stamping foot.*), Mr Wykeham, I mean —

how dare you? I'll never forgive you! I'll never forgive *any* of you, for treating Uncle Stephen like that! (*Turns to exit through window.*)

Donna Lucia (*centre, stopping* Amy, *taking her hand*): Be patient with us, my dear. Your uncle shall have the most profound reparation my influence can make.

(p. 98)

But the anxious reaction of 'Charley's Aunt' himself, whose mind continues to run on its own fixed track, sustains a comic note:

Lord Fancourt (*turning, grabs* Charley's *right arm*): Charley, can he have me up for breach of promise?

(p.97)

The absurdity of Spettigue's position cannot be forgotten, and the festive ending manages to sweep on its way.

Borrowing an opposition of terms from Anouilh, who published his plays grouped under titles which described their general spirit ('pièces roses', 'pièces noires', 'pièces brillantes' etc.), I suggest that a mild degree of empathy, as in the examples above, tends to produce farce 'en rose'. A softly romantic and festive mood allows the audience to enjoy its joking and to rest assured that contrition will duly be tendered to the offended dignities. It is equally easy, however, for empathy to swing the farcical mood in a different direction, producing farce 'en noir'. Here, the mixtures of laughter and sympathy, or the rapid alternation between the two, is brought to a halt long enough to produce the additional element which creates black humour — alarm, and even terror.

One of Marcel Marceau's most memorable pantomimes provides a striking example of this transition. It is *The Mask Maker*, which Walter Kerr describes as follows:

Here the mask maker is trying on his various masks, quickly substituting one for another. But a particularly gleeful mask, sheer grin from ear to ear, becomes stuck. The mask maker tries to remove it, but cannot. His efforts are confident at first, then increasingly desperate. In due course we know that the real face behind the mask is a thing of maddened frustration, of unadulterated anguish. But all we can see is a perpetual smile. Because M. Marceau is a mime, he is using no real masks; we are looking directly at his face, in which the two expressions, one evident, one intimated, coincide. The fusion is absolute. The comic image dominates, because Marceau is essentially a comedian; yet we see and feel clearly what is behind it, even as it does so. (*Tragedy and Comedy*, N. Y., 1967, pp.32-3)

A disguise which acquires a life and will of its own, overpowering the clever prankster who first assumed it of his own volition, is an example of the principle of tit-for-tat that takes place in the realm of fantasy. But Marceau calls attention to the fundamental human truth underlying this and all other farcical jokes — the helplessness of mankind in the face of an unpredictable universe. As long as the clown is imperturbable in defeat and disaster, laughter remains broad and uncomplicated; but when his terror begins to show, it renders our laughter more and more alarming.

Change in tempo is a technique which is powerfully exploited by the Theatre of the Absurd in the plays of Beckett, Ionesco, Pinter, Genet and others. Here, the practical joke is simply existence, which a malignant universe has apparently wished upon a variety of helpless and squirming victims, none of whom are much more than flat type-characters, endowed with symbolic significance on behalf of mankind in general. Their sufferings provide both the laughter and the horror of these plays. Ionesco actually sub-titled *Les Chaises* (1952) 'farce tragique'; and so it is. Its structure is that of a gigantic snowball which bursts with an ironic reversal and so dies in a cacophony of catcalls and hoots from an imaginary audience.

The rebels against propriety are not young lovers but a pathetic elderly couple (and he ironically a caretaker); and their attempts at indulging in sex and success are mere fantasies. The one escape which is real for them is a return to childishness; and Ionesco carefully underlines the self-pitying aspects of this with pauses and grotesque mimic play — the old woman rocking the old man on her knees, for example — until the sterility of it all is more obvious than the comedy. The couple's great scene of triumph is similarly hollow — a snowball which accumulates imaginary guests of increasing importance, up to 'the Emperor' himself, to receive from an Orator's lips a Message conceived by the old man. Chairs and more chairs are the visible substance of the snowball, as they are lined up in rows to seat guests who do not exist. At the climax, when the Orator himself arrives — by contrast a real actor — the old couple fling themselves to a watery and glorious grave before the Message begins. But the Orator is mute and has no intelligible message. By refusing to wait for the explosion of the snowball, the protagonists have avoided disillusion, but only at the cost of insisting upon the fatuity of their illusions.

Both the grotesqueness of the characterization in *Les Chaises*, and the gap between the characters' and the audience's versions of reality, tend to inhibit the establishment of empathy. The action is interrupted by frequent silences which prevent continuous laughter and allow a powerful irony to pervade the play. This is reinforced by the fact that familiar structures are inverted and arriving at an anti-climax, disappoint the audience of its expected farcical satisfactions. The result is a bitter and puzzled laughter.

When the figures of absurdism display more awareness of their predicament they naturally invite a greater degree of involvement from the audience. Beckett, in contrast to Ionesco, produces an even blacker shade of laughter for this reason: his characters draw attention to their self-consciousness. In *Endgame* (1957) for example, the symbiotic pair of Hamm, blind master, and Clov, paralytic servant, appear to be abandoned in a cellar on the last shores of a blighted earth. They are consciously reduced to performing an unending series of minor rituals — the awakening, the inspection, the medicine, the reminiscences, the story-telling, the quarrel, the threats, the running-away, the final soliloquy and the exit. They know very well that all these are merely a game — an 'Endgame' — endlessly to be repeated. Clov's threatened rebellion is restricted to hitting his master over the head with a toy dog and his desertion to standing at the door dressed for the road but making no move to leave. Their roles trap both characters just as Hamm's old parents, Nagg and Nell, are confined to their famous garbage-cans. And all the characters are trapped in their bodies, needing to eat, to pee and to look beyond their prison, even if eyes are blind. They long vaguely for 'something from the heart', and mostly for an end; but they are unwilling or unable to finish anything.

This automatism and its absurd inversion of norms produce a kind of burlesque farce which is unmistakably comic in performance. But each episode is punctuated sooner or later by a pause which signals an awareness of artifice on the part of the actors. Nagg and Nell, for example, conduct us from hilarity to pathos in their first appearance:

(Nagg *knocks on the lid of the other bin. Pause. He knocks harder. The lid lifts and the hands of* Nell *appear, gripping the rim. Then her head emerges. Lace cap. Very white face.*)

   Nell: What is it, my pet? (*Pause*) Time for love?

   Nagg: Were you asleep?

   Nell: Oh no!

   Nagg: Kiss me.

   Nell: We can't.

   Nagg: Try.

     (*Their heads strain towards each other, fail to meet, fall apart again.*)

Nell: Why this farce, day after day?
   (*Pause.*)

                                    (*Endgame*, N.Y., 1958, p. 14.)

Pressure on the laughing audience is exerted in this way time after time. Clov, ascending a step-ladder with a telescope in a ridiculous clown-sequence of mistakes and confusion, attacks directly when the audience roars with laughter:

Clov: Things are livening up.
   (*He gets up on the ladder, raises the telescope, lets it fall.*)
   I did it on purpose.
   (*He gets down, picks up the telescope, turns it on the auditorium.*) I see . . . a multitude . . . in transports . . . of joy.
   (*Pause.*) That's what I call a magnifier.
   (*He lowers the telescope, turns towards* Hamm.) Well?
   Don't we laugh?
Hamm (*after reflection*): I don't.
Clov (*after reflection*): Nor I.   (p.29)

The laugher finds himself accused of participation in this practical joke. He is contributing to the anguish of the victim on stage; and since the joke is that which is played on all mankind, he is obliged to suffer with the victim. At the same time, the deterioration of normal speech, of customary plot, and of comprehensible motivation on the part of the inhabitants of this world is so marked that an audience must constantly question any real identification with them. For Martin Esslin, this permits the Theatre of the Absurd to be 'a comic theatre in spite of the fact that its subject matter is sombre, violent, and bitter . . . it transcends the categories of comedy and tragedy and combines laughter with horror' (*The Theatre of the Absurd*, p.361).

   The horror of absurdism does not come from the violent acts which characterize the related Theatre of Cruelty of Arrabal and Artaud. It derives from the helplessness of the victims and the relentlessness of the powers which tease them. It is the horror of the practical joke. Ionesco, describing his own work and its techniques in *Notes and Counter-Notes* (trans. Donald Watson, N.Y., 1964), wrote:

> It was not for me to conceal the devices of the theatre, but rather make them still more evident, deliberately obvious, go all out for caricature and the grotesque, way beyond the pale irony of witty drawing-room comedies. No drawing-room comedies, but farce, the extreme exaggeration of parody. Humor, yes, but using the methods of burlesque. Comic effects that are firm, broad and outrageous. No dramatic comedies either. But back to the unendurable. Everything raised to paroxysm, where the source of tragedy lies. A theatre of violence; violently comic, violently dramatic. (p.26)

This, as A.P. Hinchliffe points out elsewhere in this series, is 'one of the ways of facing up to a universe that has lost its meaning and purpose' (*The Absurd*, London, 1969, p.11).

Ionesco was surprised to recognize the similarities between his approach and that of Feydeau, to whose plays his attention was called by the comments of several reviewers. In the introduction to his translation of four Feydeau plays, Norman Shapiro describes how both dramatists are concerned with 'the projection, in theatrical terms, of the aimlessness and unpredictability of man's fate in a haphazard (or, at least, inexplicable) universe, in which things — mainly bad — will happen to him for no obvious or compelling reason. In this sense, there is a good dose of "absurdity" in Feydeau' (*Four Farces by Georges Feydeau*, Chicago, 1972, p.xlv). The difference between the two dramatic projections is one of focus. Ionesco is openly concerned with the helpless condition of his victims; Feydeau with their frantic, if mostly ill-fated, efforts to compromise with the machine. Whereas in the Theatre of the Absurd, frenetic activity alternates with the silence of resignation; in Feydeau, the characters are far too involved in their frenzy to pause for self-contemplation.

Nevertheless, at the conclusion of a Feydeau farce, in the aftertaste of the evening's entertainment or in reflection after reading a play to its end, an element of doubt begins to make itself felt. The sheer madness of the pace — the violence of comic effect of which Ionesco speaks — and the casual hurts inflicted not only upon the principals of the piece but also upon reasonably harmless bystanders, as well as the extraordinary callousness of all the characters in their relationships with one another — all these begin to add up to a rather nasty portrait of human nature. One feels that, despite the impersonal nature of the comic mechanisms at work — coincidence, snowballing confusions, interferences and reversals — the collective selfish egos of the victims are to blame for their problems.

Feydeau himself was well aware of the ambivalent relationship between suffering and laughter. He once explained to his son, Michel, that to create laughter one should take any group of people and place them in a tragic situation and attempt to view them from a comic angle. In his earlier plays with their complex reversals and counter-reversals, pity is usually taken upon those outsiders who have been inadvertently dragged into suffering and humiliation. Shapiro points out in the introduction cited above that the audience is given to understand that reparation will duly be made. In his last plays, however, Feydeau rejected these extended circular structures in favour of the concentrated form of the deadlocked quarrel-farce. The effect, as we have seen in the farces of Chapter 3, can be quite claustrophobic.

Between 1908 and his final play, *Hortense a dit "Je m'en fous!" (Hortense said, 'I Don't Give a Damn!'*, 1916), Feydeau created a series of five one-act farces, which he apparently intended to publish collectively under the title *Du Marriage au divorce (From Marriage to Divorce)*. Here, as in Courteline's *Les Boulingrin*, the spouses are locked in a combat which is as deadly as it is comic and from which no escape is offered. The principle at work is that of the eternal counterpoise, the 'balan-

cier' effect discussed in Chapter 3: movement in one direction
immediately produces countervailing movement to restore the
balance.

Feydeau's husbands are as anxious to be well-mannered as
was M. Boulingrin. They are professional men, concerned to
keep up appearance before their clients, their guests, and their
domestics. But they are hopelessly henpecked. In *Hortense*,
the dentist Follbraguet is advised by his receptionist, Adrien,
to exercise his legal rights and demand that his wife apologize
to Hortense, her maid. Greatly daring (and under the ridiculous threat of having to fight a duel over Hortense's honour if
he does not), he tries:

> *Follbraguet (to his wife,* Marcelle): . . . and, anyway, that's
> an end of the matter. I am the master here and I demand
> that you do it.
> (Adrien *appears in the doorway and stops to listen.*)
> *Marcelle*: Ah! 'You demand it!' Take that! (*She slaps him.*)
> *Follbraguet*: Oh!
> *Marcelle*: Monsieur demands it! (*She exits left.*)
> *Follbraguet (to* Adrien): Well, there you are, my friend,
> when I try to exercise my authority, that's what happens!
> (Sc. viii, *Théâtre Complet*, vol. I, my translation, 1948,
> p.248)

The quarrel goes from bad to worse; and, as Follbraguet
works distractedly on his last suffering patient for the day — a
Monsieur Vildamour — he can hear his wife off-stage deliberately countermanding the orders he has given to the servants.
He alternates distractedly between his patient and the door,
until Madame bursts in and the last scene is played out before
the bewildered eyes of the patient bound and gagged in the dentist's chair. Madame intends to leave. Monsieur also will leave
and Madame is welcome to his practice and his patients:

> *Follbraguet*: Go on, do the work instead of me!
> *Marcelle*: Me!

Vildamour (*terrified by the prospect*): Oh no!

Marcelle: Not likely! It's all very well for you! To have to poke my fingers into all these disgusting old mouths — the thought is absolutely revolting!

Follbraguet (*as he furiously strips off his gown and puts on his jacket, which he takes down from its peg, together with his hat*): Maybe, but that doesn't hinder the fact that thanks to these disgusting old mouths (*instinctively gesturing towards* Vildamour) that I put my hands into, I am able to pay for all your clothes and the 'frills and more frills and more frills again'. Now you can arrange to earn all that for yourself: me, I'm bowing out!

Marcelle: Just as you please! Only, I warn you, you needn't expect to find me still in this house tonight!

Follbraguet: And me neither! Goodbye! (*He exits at rear.*)

Marcelle: Goodbye! (*She exits left.*)

Vildamour: (*who has followed the conclusion of this dialogue in anguish, raising himself and in panic at finding himself abandoned with all the equipment still in his mouth*): Oh no! Oh no! Oh no!

CURTAIN   (p.252)

Like des Rillettes in *Les Boulingrin*, Vildamour has become the target for violence deflected from one spouse to the other. But, unlike the other, he is scarcely responsible for his own fate. Visiting his dentist, he is surely entitled to professional help, not a domestic maelstrom. It is not a large step from this farcical situation to the existentialist point of view that hell is other people. As Ionesco puts it, 'Social man is hell; other people are hell; if only one could do without them!' (*Cahiers des Saisons*, XV, Winter 1959, pp.262-7). For the warring spouses, this is undoubtedly true — their torments will continue as long as they remain bound to their partner in marriage. Peace can be bought only by submission, or by the kind of growth in character that farce-structures are designed to exclude. In the undertow of pity for poor Vildamour and in the brilliant clarity of Feydeau's analysis of selfishness, an audience must surely deepen its understanding of human folly. If this is so, then farce at its blackest may create an implicit kindliness: it points to the possibilities of renewal and reconciliation beyond its own boundaries.

For Feydeau, it seems rather to have precipitated insanity and death; but his gift to his audiences was immense. J.L. Styan has asserted that 'love and marriage, social forms and other familiar matters are immediately visible in a new way through farce. Its clockwork mechanism by its very consistency disarms us. In its spirit of violence and riot, no doubt we should recognize that hidden depths of the mind are being revealed' (*Drama, Stage and Audience*, p.83). Despite its gaiety, despite its cruelty, farce is a serious theatrical genre.

Suggestions for further reading

For general reading on the subject of farce. Eric Bentley's essay on 'The Psychology of Farce' (*'Let's Get a Divorce!' And Other Plays,* N.Y., 1958) and Leo Hughes' *A Century of English Farce* (Princeton, N.J., 1956) are important, and Bentley's *The Life of the Drama* (N.Y., 1964) includes a chapter on farce (pp.219-56) which expands on his earlier essay. Walter Kerr's *Tragedy and Comedy* (N.Y., 1967) also provides some interesting insights into the spirit of farce (although he prefers to designate the genre as 'low comedy'). The Freudian approach in Morton Gurewitch's *Comedy: the Irrational Vision* is highly over-simplified. Readers interested in Freud's analysis of joking would do better to turn to Freud himself, in *Jokes and their Relation to the Unconscious* (trans. James Strachey, London, 1960); or to a paper by Paul Kline, 'The Psychoanalytic Theory of Humour and Laughter', in *It's a Funny Thing, Humour* (ed. A.J. Chapman and H.C. Foot, Oxford, 1977), which briefly expounds Freudian theory on this subject.

The theatricality and stylization of farce are dealt with by J.L. Styan in his general discussion of dramatic perspective, *Drama, Stage and Audience* (Cambridge, 1975). Henri Bergson's much under-rated monograph, *Le Rire* (originally published Geneva, 1945) is worth reading for its insights into the structural devices of farce in performance: it is translated in *Comedy* (ed. Wylie Sypher, N.Y., 1956). A convenient collection of many critical writings on comedy — including Bentley's essay and that by Vsevolod Meyerhold entitled 'Farce' — is

R.W. Corrigan's anthology, *Comedy: Meaning and Form* (San Francisco, 1965).

Very few books deal exclusively with farce, although many studies of comedy touch incidentally on the subject. Perhaps the most rewarding approach to further reading is to focus upon the texts and background of a particular period. Some of the most accessible are:

Classical and Italian farce

Bentley, Eric (ed.), *The Classic Theatre, Vol. I: Six Italian Plays*, N.Y., 1958. Includes an 'English version' of *The Three Cuckolds*, as well as examples of eighteenth-century treatments of the comedy of masks by Goldoni and Gozzi.

Lea, Kathleen M., *Italian Popular Comedy: A study in the commedia dell'arte 1560-1620, with special reference to the English stage*, 2 vols, Oxford, 1934. Highly detailed; volume 2 includes several typical scenarii, including the original *Li Tre Becchi (The Three Cuckolds)*, in English and Italian parallel texts.

Nicoll, Allardyce M., *The World of Harlequin*, London, 1963. The history and characters of the *commedia dell'arte*, with generous illustrations.

Nicoll, Allardyce M., *Masks, Mimes and Miracles*, N.Y., 1963. Fully illustrated account of the traces of mimic farce in the classical world and the early Middle Ages.

Oreglia, Giacomo, *The Commedia dell'Arte*, trans. L.F. Edwards, London, 1968. An excellent, concise account of the *commedia*, with representative texts and illustrations.

Plautus, trans. E.F. Watling, *The Pot of Gold and Other Plays*, Harmondsworth, 1965. Includes the *Menaechmi (Brothers Menaechmus)*.

Plautus, trans. E.F. Watling, *The Rope and Other Plays*, Harmondsworth, 1964. Includes the *Mostellaria (Haunted House)*.

Segal, Erich, *Roman Laughter: The comedy of Plautus*, Cambridge, Mass., 1968. Lively study of Plautine comedy in relation to Roman society.

French Mediaeval farce and Molière

Attinger, Gustave, *L'Esprit de la commedia dell'arte dans le théâtre français*, Paris, 1950. Succinct account of Italian influence upon French comedy and farce; includes as a preface an excellent description of the techniques of mime and type-character.

Bermel, Albert (trans. and ed.), *One-Act Comedies of Molière*, Cleveland, Ohio, 1965. Unusual selection of the short farces in racy translations; includes *Le Cocu imaginaire*.

Bowen, Barbara M., *Les Caractéristiques essentielles de la farce française et leur survivance dans les années 1550-1620*, Urbana, 1964. A complete historical survey, supplemented by the author's earlier article, 'Towards the Definition of Farce as a Literary "Genre"', in *Modern Languages Review*, LVI, 1961, pp.558-60, on the distinction between the *farce* and the *sottie*.

Bowen, Barbara (ed.), *Four Farces*, Oxford, 1967. French texts include *Le Cuvier* and *Maître Pierre Pathelin*.

Brereton, Geoffrey, *French Comic Drama from the Sixteenth to the Eighteenth Century*, London, 1977. An excellent general survey.

Denny, Neville (ed.), *Medieval Interludes*, London, 1972. Includes lively versions of *The Olives*, by Lope de Rueda, Heywood's *John John*, and Hans Sachs' *The Wandering Scholar from Paradise*, as well as a French *farce* and a Flemish *sotternie*, all in English translation.

Lancaster, Henry Carrington (ed.), *Five French Farces, 1655-1694(?)*, Baltimore, 1937. A scholarly edition of French texts from the post-Molière period by the leading historian of French classical drama.

Lanson, Gustave, 'Molière et la farce', in *Révue de Paris*, III, 1901, pp.129-53. Translated by Ruby Cohn as 'Molière and

Farce', in *Tulane Drama Review*, VIII, 1963, pp.133-54.

Mandel, Oscar (trans. and ed.), *Five Comedies of Medieval France*, N.Y., 1970. Free, but readable, translations of both Le Cuvier and *Maître Pierre Pathelin*.

Maxwell, Ian, *French Farce and John Heywood*, Melbourne, 1946. Excellent account of French mediaeval *farce* as a genre and of Heywood's debt to specific French texts.

Molière, Jean-Baptiste Poquelin, *The Miser and Other Plays*, and *The Misanthrope and Other Plays*, trans. John Wood, Harmondsworth, 1962 and 1959.

Tissier, André, *La Farce en France de 1450 à 1550*, 2 vols, Paris, 1976. Benefits from recent scholarship and from the inclusion of several farce-texts, among them the *Farce du Cuvier*.

Elizabethan and Restoration farce

Barber, Cesar Lombard, *Shakespeare's Festive Comedy: A study of dramatic form and its relation to social custom*, Princeton, N.J., 1959. Concerned with the tradition of festive licence and its reflection in Shakespearean comedy.

Baskervill, Charles Read, *The Elizabethan Jig and Related Song-Drama*, Chicago, 1929; reprinted N.Y., 1965. Dense and highly detailed account of the jigs and jig-makers. Includes the few surviving texts, some in their Low German versions, others in English.

Bevis, Richard W. (ed.), *Eighteenth-Century Drama: After-pieces*, Oxford, 1970. A critical edition of assorted after-pieces, ranging from farce to satire, with a useful introduction on the history and functions of the double-bill. Includes *Miss in her Teens* by Garrick.

Donaldson, Ian, *The World Upside Down: Comedy from Jonson to Fielding*, Oxford, 1970. Does not treat farce as such, but discusses the themes of social inversion and satire inherited by English dramatists from pre-Christian rituals and beliefs.

Gurr, Andrew, *The Shakespearean Stage, 1574-1642,* Cambridge, 1970. Provides a readable summary of the known facts about the stage-jig, pp.113-15.

Hughes, Leo, *A Century of English Farce*, Princeton, N.J., 1956. An invaluable account of the fortunes of farce following the re-opening of the theatres in 1660. Includes a thoughtful discussion of farce as a genre and its theatrical techniques.

Hughes, Leo and A.H. Scouten (eds), *Ten English Farces*, Austin, Texas, 1948. A companion volume to that above: texts from the Restoration to mid-eighteenth century. Also includes *Miss in her Teens*.

Salingar, Leo, *Shakespeare and the Traditions of Comedy*, Cambridge, 1974. Ranges widely over the styles and types of comedy — including farce — passed on from the classical world to the theatres of the Renaissance.

Nineteenth-century farce in France and England

Bentley, Eric (ed.), '*Let's Get a Divorce' and Other Plays*, N.Y., 1958. Selection of French farces, including Bentley's translation of *Les Boulingrin* by Courteline (as *These Cornfields!*). His essay on 'The Psychology of Farce' prefaces the volume, pp.vii-xx.

Booth, Michael R., 'Early Victorian Farce: Dionysus domesticated', in *Nineteenth-Century British Theatre*, ed K. Richards and P. Thomson, London, 1971. pp.95-110. Discusses a selection of 'domestic' farces — including *Box and Cox* — and their themes.

Booth, Michael R. (ed.), '*The Magistrate' and Other Nineteenth-Century Plays*, Oxford, 1974. Prints *Box and Cox* and another 'domestic' farce to contrast with the more 'Parisian' farce by Pinero, *The Magistrate*. The introduction provides useful historical background, pp.xviii-xx.

Davies, Frederick (trans.), *Three French Farces*, Harmondsworth, 1973. Labiche, Sardou and Feydeau in read-able translations, with an introduction which tackles the vexed question of how much the prolific *farceurs* owe to their assorted collaborators and joint-authors.

Meyer, Peter (trans.), *Three Farces of Georges Feydeau*, London, 1974. Translations prepared for the BBC's productions of *Tailleur pour dames (Fitting for Ladies), Champignol malgré lui (A Close Shave)*, and *Le Dindon (Sauce for the Goose)*.

Mortimer, John (trans.), *A Flea in her Ear*, London, 1968. Translation of *La Puce à l'oreille*, prepared for the National Theatre production in 1967.

Shapiro, Norman R. (trans.), *Four Farces by Georges Feydeau*, Chicago, 1970. Includes an excellent introduction on the theatre and times of Feydeau.

Taylor, John Russell, *The Rise and Fall of the Well-Made Play*, London, 1967. Account of the structural principles in the work of the French farce-writers during the nineteenth century, from Scribe to Labiche, Courteline and Feydeau. Pinero's debt to French farce is also discussed.

Contemporary versions of farce

Esslin, Martin, *The Theatre of the Absurd*, rev. edn., Garden City, N.J., 1969. Still the standard work, updated to include dramatists such as N.F. Simpson.

Kerr, Walter, *The Silent Clowns*, N.Y., 1975. A thorough discussion of the era of farce in silent film; includes many stills.

Lamont, Rosette, 'The Metaphysical Farce: Beckett and Ionesco' in *French Review*, XXXIII, February 1959, pp.319-28. This deals specifically with the issues raised in Chapter 5 of this book.

Taylor, J.R., *The Second Wave*, N.Y., 1971. Includes a brief discussion of dramatist Alan Ayckbourn, as a contemporary farce-writer.

Index